I0605946

Flourish
Daily Devotions
for Teen Girls

Flourish

Daily Devotions for Teen Girls

BARBOUR
PUBLISHING

ISBN 979-8-89151-079-1

Text compiled from *Choose Courage*, *Choose Confidence*, *Choose Jesus*, *Choose Prayer*, *Choose Love,* and *Choose Kindness*, all published by Barbour Publishing, Inc.

Published by Barbour Publishing, Inc., 1810 Barbour Drive, Uhrichsville, Ohio 44683, www.barbourbooks.com

Our mission is to inspire the world with the life-changing message of the Bible.

Printed in China.

You Can Flourish in Your Faith!

Do you desire to know God better? To find strength in Him? To see your faith grow deeper? Spending time with the Lord in prayer and Bible reading is the best way to flourish in your relationship with Him.

These 365 daily devotions will guide you through just-right-sized readings you can experience in as few as three minutes:

- Minute 1: Reflect on God's Word
- Minute 2: Read real-life application and encouragement
- Minute 3: Pray

Consider these devotions as a jump start to help you form a habit of spending time with God every day. Think about what you learn and share insights with friends, family, and others you come in contact with every day. They're looking for inspiration and encouragement. . .how to flourish. . .too.

> "But blessed are those who trust in the Lord
> and have made the Lord their hope and confidence.
> They are like trees planted along a riverbank,
> with roots that reach deep into the water.
> Such trees are not bothered by the heat or
> worried by long months of drought. Their leaves
> stay green, and they never stop producing fruit."
> Jeremiah 17:7–8 NLT

Day 1

Love Goes On Forever

All the special gifts and powers from God will someday come to an end, but love goes on forever. Someday prophecy and speaking in unknown languages and special knowledge—these gifts will disappear.

1 Corinthians 13:8 TLB

What a great reminder that love will last forever. There is nothing that can stop it from infiltrating the lives of those who follow the Lord. It's seared into our DNA, unable to die away. While everything else will eventually fade away—including the gifts and powers that come from God to our earthly lives—love never will.

Friend, what is the Holy Spirit speaking into your heart right now? Is love alive and active, or are you allowing bitterness to take root? Are hard moments and difficult people robbing you of warm and fuzzy feelings in other areas? Are you losing joy for this life, sinking into the pit of despair?

Let God reignite the love that's faded. God says it will go on forever, so ask Him to make it so!

Lord, love feels faint these days.
Help it burn bright in me once again. Amen.

Day 2

About Love

Dear friends, let us love one another, for love comes from God. Everyone who loves has been born of God and knows God. Whoever does not love does not know God, because God is love.

1 John 4:7–8 NIV

It's easy to say we love everyone in a generic, standoffish way. After all, we don't want bad things to happen to anyone. But loving the person who hates you. . .being kind to the sibling who annoys you. . .showing patience to the person who drives you crazy. . .those things take self-discipline. They also take courage in a world where sarcasm and cancel culture are encouraged.

But you are God's strong, courageous daughter. You are made in His image, and He is love. When love is hard, lean into Him. Ask Him for strength. He will help you be kind, compassionate, and humble. He will help you love when love isn't the natural response.

Help me love like You love, Father.
When my first response is anger or
impatience or sarcasm, intervene.
Teach me to respond to others as You do.

Day 3

The Beginning of Sin

Everyone has sinned; we all fall short of God's glorious standard.

Romans 3:23 NLT

When God created everything, including the first two people, Adam and Eve, He didn't make them robots programmed to do His bidding. He gave them free will—the ability to choose to love Him and obey His good guidance or not. He wants love and devotion from people that is chosen and real, not forced and fake. Adam and Eve chose to disobey Him, and ever since, sin has been spreading everywhere. And there's a big price to pay for sin: suffering and death. But God still loved people in spite of sin, and He knew we would need a way to choose to be right with Him again. So He sent Jesus to be our Savior.

Father God, You are Creator, and You are perfect! Thank You for loving people in spite of all our sin. Thank You for sending Your Son, Jesus, and giving me and all people the free will to choose Him! Amen.

Day 4

Calm Confidence

This is what the Sovereign LORD, the Holy One of Israel, says: "Only in returning to me and resting in me will you be saved. In quietness and confidence is your strength."

ISAIAH 30:15 NLT

Daily you face the choice: *Where will I put my confidence—in God, myself, or someone else?* Are you looking to God to save you? Do you rely on yourself to get through? Or do you put all your hope in someone else, believing that person will save you? The Israelites said, "No, we will get our help from Egypt. They will give us swift horses for riding into battle" (Isaiah 30:16 NLT). They refused to rest in God's care for them, to calmly trust God for protection and deliverance. They took matters into their own hands and placed their confidence elsewhere. But our true strength lies in our calm trust in Jesus. What problems do you face today? Choose confidence in God.

Lord, today I choose to put my confidence in You, not in myself and not in others. Help me face today in calmness and peace as I depend on You to care for me.

Day 5

God's Friend

And the scripture was fulfilled that says, "Abraham believed God, and it was credited to him as righteousness," and he was called God's friend.

JAMES 2:23 NIV

Friendship is important. The best friends are those who like you just the way you are, who treat you like you're important, and who make a habit of building you up.

God is the best friend we could ever hope for. He does all those things and more. And though He loves everyone, there's a way we can get in extra tight with Him. When we trust God and believe His promises. . .when we spend time getting to know Him—talking to Him and reading His Word. . .those things please God. When we show Him we love Him and trust Him with all our heart, He brings us close, into His "in-crowd," and calls us His friend.

I love You more than anything, Lord. You are my best friend. I want to live in a way that makes me Your friend too.

Day 6

To Be Kind

She opens her mouth with wisdom,
and the teaching of kindness is on her tongue.
PROVERBS 31:26 ESV

What does it mean to be kind? And what does a life of kindness look like?

A kind person seeks the well-being of others through their words, attitude, and actions. A kind person learns to value peace and harmony over retaliation and anger. A kind person listens quickly, speaks gently, and loves fiercely. A kind person shows mercy and compassion to anyone in need.

You won't accidentally stumble into a life of kindness. It's a path that must be chosen and traveled carefully. A life of kindness takes determination, discipline, and grace. When you choose kindness, Jesus shines through your life, beckoning the world to a hope greater than anything found on this earth.

Dear Lord, I want to choose kindness. Send Your Spirit to fill me with kindness so that other people might come to know You.

Day 7

Extraordinary Love

"This is how much God loved the world: He gave his Son, his one and only Son. And this is why: so that no one need be destroyed; by believing in him, anyone can have a whole and lasting life."

John 3:16 MSG

Can you imagine the grit it took for God to give up His Son to death on a cross? He watched as Christ suffered. God saw the persecution. He witnessed the injustices that came His way. And because God chose love, His one and only Son, Jesus, stepped out of heaven and into the world to save us. Now that is love, friend. That is how much God values you.

Today, meditate on that sacrificial decision of compassion for us. Talk to the Lord, sharing your gratitude. Express your thankful heart for His willingness to choose love on your behalf. What a beautiful example of selflessness we can show others by how we treat them.

Let's choose to love in extraordinary ways too. With God's help, we can let others know how much they matter through the words we share and the actions we take.

Lord, help me show others extraordinary love. Amen.

Day 8

Calling on His Name

To Seth also a son was born; and he named him Enosh.
Then people began to call upon the name of the Lord.
Genesis 4:26 NASB

Adam and Eve were the first man and woman to be created by God. Genesis explains that in the garden of Eden, Adam and Eve walked with God and talked with God, and it was very good.

Once they sinned, though, their perfect conversations with the Lord were forever changed. And once Adam and Eve had children, their sons didn't obey the Lord. In fact, Cain killed his brother Abel.

Adam and Eve's grandson Enosh would've heard about his grandparents' relationship with God in the garden. When Enosh was alive, people began to call upon the name of the Lord. That means they prayed.

Just like these early people felt compelled to approach the Lord, you can call upon His name too. As you seek Him, call on His name!

Lord, I am so grateful I can call on You!
Thank You that You welcome me to approach You.

Day 9

Safety and Unity

"I am coming to you; I will not stay in the world any longer. But they are still in the world. Holy Father, keep them safe by the power of your name, the name you gave me, so that they will be one, just as you and I are one."

John 17:11 NCV

When Jesus knew His death was nearing, He prayed for His disciples and for followers who would come in future years. In other words, He was praying for you!

How did Jesus pray for you? He prayed you'd be kept safe in this world by the power of God's holy name. He also prayed for unity of believers.

To echo Jesus' prayer, don't be afraid to ask God to keep you safe. When you find yourself disagreeing with another Christ follower, pray about your disagreement. Ask God to help unite you together as the body of Christ.

Holy Father, what a gift that Jesus prayed for me! Like He prayed, please keep me safe by the power of Your name. Please help me be united with other believers so that we may be one just like You and Jesus are one.

Day 10

Jesus Makes Us Right with God

We are made right with God by placing our faith in Jesus Christ. And this is true for everyone who believes, no matter who we are. For everyone has sinned; we all fall short of God's glorious standard. Yet God, in his grace, freely makes us right in his sight. He did this through Christ Jesus when he freed us from the penalty for our sins. For God presented Jesus as the sacrifice for sin.

ROMANS 3:22–25 NLT

Like Adam and Eve, we choose bad behavior and disobedience to God sometimes in our own unique ways. We hurt others. We act rude. We say mean things. We lie or cheat in big or small ways. We get jealous. The list goes on and on. But the Father who made us, the one true Creator God, is perfect. We all need relationship with Him. And the only way to be right with Him and have relationship with Him is through Jesus Christ, whom He sent to pay the price for our sin.

Jesus, thank You that You make it possible to be right with God because You died on the cross to pay for my sin. Amen.

Day 11

What's Your Source?

Whom have I in heaven but you? And earth has nothing I desire besides you. My flesh and my heart may fail, but God is the strength of my heart and my portion forever.
PSALM 73:25–26 NIV

It's way too easy to be confident because of your looks, abilities, friends, followers, possessions, or anything else that makes you feel valued. Don't be tricked so easily! The source of your confidence is more important than your actual confidence. Placing your confidence in yourself or the things of this world will always let you down because those sources are unreliable. Place your trust in Jesus. Gain your confidence from Him. He will always be with you and never let you down. His strength will more than make up for what you lack. Be confident because you are created with the image of God stamped on you, because you are loved by God, because God knows you are beautiful, and because you have perfect protection, peace, and power in Him.

Lord, show me where I'm drawing my confidence from people or places other than You. Help me shift my focus to You as my source.

Day 12

Words

Those who consider themselves religious and yet do not keep a tight rein on their tongues deceive themselves, and their religion is worthless.

JAMES 1:26 NIV

There's an old rhyme that says, "Sticks and stones may break my bones, but words will never hurt me." Whoever wrote that had never been the target of mean insults or cruel gossip. Bruises heal, but unkind words stay in a person's memory. They sink into our spirits, replay in our thoughts, and cause pain for years—even decades.

We can't always control what enters our minds. But we do have the power to edit those thoughts before we speak them out loud. God is love, and He wants us to be love too. Next time you're tempted to say something unkind or cruel or impatient, take a deep breath. Ask God to form your words for you. Then choose to speak always and only with love.

Help me control my words, Father. I want my speech to build others up, not tear them down. I want all my words to reflect Your love.

Day 13

Join Others in What They're Feeling

Be happy with those who are happy, and weep with those who weep.
ROMANS 12:15 NLT

Imagine you have incredibly exciting news—you got the lead in the school play, you're going on an awesome vacation, or you won concert tickets to see your favorite singer. When you tell your friend your news though, her response is simply "That's cool," and then she changes the subject.

Now imagine you're having a tough day. You tell your friend that you're sad and anxious, and her response is simply "But you have so many good things in your life. Focus on those instead of being sad!"

Hopefully, your friends respond better than that, because one expression of kindness is joining others in what they're feeling. By celebrating with someone when something amazing happens or quietly sitting next to them and listening when they're sad, we visibly show the love of Jesus.

Dear Lord, please give me the ability to notice when others are going through something and to join them in their celebration or sadness.

Day 14

Being Kind and Loving

But if a person isn't loving and kind, it shows that he doesn't know God—for God is love.

1 John 4:8 TLB

Whoa. This is a big scriptural statement! It tells us that how we treat others reveals our heart for God. It uncovers the truth of our faith. And it's a fantastic reminder that because God *is* love, we have access to a deep well of it to lavish on others. Are you choosing to do so?

Every day we get to decide how we will act toward others. We get to determine how we treat our parents, our siblings, our friends, our teachers, our teammates, and those we meet on the street. We can be kind, or we can be mean. We can be loving, or we can be hateful. It's our choice. But because we know God and follow His ways, we can ask for help so we're a blessing to those around us. We can choose to be kind and loving, even when it feels impossible.

Lord, help my actions toward others to reflect my faith. Amen.

Day 15

Jesus Is Our Only Savior from Sin

For the sin of this one man, Adam, caused death to rule over many. But even greater is God's wonderful grace and his gift of righteousness, for all who receive it will live in triumph over sin and death through this one man, Jesus Christ.

Romans 5:17 NLT

Jesus willingly gave up His life on the cross and died to pay for our sin. When we admit our sin and trust in Him as our Savior, we are given the most amazing gift of grace, which covers our sin, plus new life that lasts forever. We begin our new life in Christ as soon as we allow Him to be our Lord and choose to follow and obey Him.

Jesus, I know I'm a sinner, and I'm sorry. I need Your forgiveness and grace. Thank You for dying on the cross to pay the penalty for my sin. Thank You that You rose to life again. Thank You for freedom from sin and for the promise of eternal life. Thank You for making me right with God. I choose You, and I choose to live for You, Jesus. Amen.

Day 16

The Choice

Jesus said to all of them, "If people want to follow me, they must give up the things they want. They must be willing to give up their lives daily to follow me."
LUKE 9:23 NCV

Jesus requires that we give up everything to follow Him. That's a hard request. Why do people willingly do that? It seems crazy! But when you are so confident in someone, you're willing to make sacrifices. You're certain what you will gain is far better than what you will lose. You're fully confident that Jesus is someone you can trust.

Do you have that confidence in Jesus? Do you know Him well enough that you're willing to trust Him with everything? When daily decisions require you to choose between your way and God's way, how often do you sacrifice what you want for what God wants? At times God's way seems hard and scary. That's when we must *choose* confidence. Knowing God's character gives us the confidence we need to walk in faith and obedience.

Jesus, I'm not gonna lie: You ask a lot of me. Help me know You better so I can follow You with total confidence.

Day 17

God Confidence

For you have been my hope, Sovereign LORD,
my confidence since my youth.
PSALM 71:5 NIV

Your parents, coaches, and teachers may tell you to have confidence in yourself. It's important to be confident and self-assured. It's important to hold your head up and shoulders back and to look people in the eye when you talk to them. But even the most capable person will mess up sometimes. None of us is perfect.

Confidence placed in God is well placed because He never messes up. He is all-powerful and all-knowing, and He always keeps His promises. And He lives in us! Take your self-confidence up a notch, and turn it into God-confidence. Stay close to Him. Seek Him every day, and live in His presence. When you face difficult things, recall the hope and confidence you have in the one who created you and who loves you more than life. He has your back!

I place all my hope and confidence in You, Father.
I know You'll take care of me no matter what.

Day 18

Show Me What I Should Do

Tell me in the morning about your love, because I trust you. Show me what I should do, because my prayers go up to you.
Psalm 143:8 NCV

Life is confusing! No matter how old you get, you'll always be faced with some decisions that leave you feeling confused.

The amazing comfort is that you don't have to worry about figuring everything out on your own, because you can ask your heavenly Father! He's the giver of all good gifts, including wisdom. Wisdom is necessary when the choice you need to make doesn't seem so simple.

Instead of expecting God to make your decision clear right away, ask Him to show you what you should do. Then pay careful attention to the situations in your life and the truth you might hear over and over in different ways. As you listen for God to answer your prayers, He'll show you what you should do.

Father, I do trust You.
Please show me what I should do!

Day 19

Showing Deep Love

Most important of all, continue to show deep love for each other, for love makes up for many of your faults.
1 PETER 4:8 TLB

How can you show deep love to others? Maybe it's obeying your parents when your heart's desire is set on something else. Maybe it's spending time with a sibling, making them a priority in your busy schedule. Maybe it's being a respectful student to your teachers, even if everyone else is being dismissive. Or maybe it's befriending the new kid who is struggling to fit in.

Be intentional to be the kind of girl who cares about the feelings of others. Take the time to choose to love in a world that doesn't seem to do that well anymore. Through your faith, you have the power to make a difference in the lives of others by simply showing compassion and care. Be the one who decides to live that way.

Lord, forgive me for the times I've not shown deep love toward others. Starting today, open my eyes and heart to the idea of embracing the power of love to those around me. Amen.

Day 20

Spiritual Clothes

Therefore, as God's chosen people, holy and dearly loved, clothe yourselves with compassion, kindness, humility, gentleness and patience.

COLOSSIANS 3:12 NIV

How much time does it take you to pick out what to wear in the morning? (Or in the afternoon on school breaks and weekends!)

As you're thinking about how to dress your physical body each day, reflect on how to clothe yourself spiritually. How can you put on kindness, compassion, humility, gentleness, and patience today?

Dear God, it's so easy to only focus on my outer appearance. Help me remember to clothe myself spiritually.

Day 21

Choose Jesus, Choose the Holy Spirit

[Jesus said:] "The Helper is the Holy Spirit. The Father will send Him in My place. He will teach you everything and help you remember everything I have told you."

JOHN 14:26 NLV

After Jesus died, He rose and returned to heaven, but God didn't just leave us alone in the world. He gave us the Holy Spirit. When you choose Jesus as Savior and Lord of your life, you receive the Holy Spirit into your life. The Holy Spirit is your comforter, your counselor, your guide, and so much more. The Holy Spirit cares for you and even prays for you when you don't know what to pray. (See Romans 8:26–28 for more about that!)

Jesus, I'm so glad You are always with me through the presence of the Holy Spirit. I am never alone, never forgotten, never without Your help and hope. Help me to sense Your Holy Spirit every single moment, in every single thing I do, and help me to listen well to Your wisdom and leading. Amen.

Day 22

I Am

Moses said to God, "Suppose I go to the Israelites and say to them, 'The God of your fathers has sent me to you,' and they ask me, 'What is his name?' Then what shall I tell them?" God said to Moses, "I AM WHO I AM. This is what you are to say to the Israelites: 'I AM has sent me to you.'"

EXODUS 3:13–14 NIV

Names meant a lot in ancient times. They reflected the character and nature of the person (Genesis 17:5–6; 32:27–28; Matthew 16:17–18). When Moses asked for God's name, he was asking, "How do You define Yourself?" God said His name is Yahweh, which means "I am who I am," indicating God is not bound by time. He is eternal and independent of all creation. He always was, is, and will be (Revelation 1:8).

Our culture prefers to define God by its own terms. People choose whatever version of God is easiest to accept. But we must allow God to define Himself by what He has revealed in the Bible.

Lord, please reveal Yourself—who You really are—to me.

Day 23

Rescuer

"Call upon Me on the day of trouble;
I will rescue you, and you will honor Me."
PSALM 50:15 NASB

When you think of a day of trouble, what comes to mind? Maybe you recall being a bully's target. Or perhaps you made a bad grade on your report card and dreaded telling your parents. It could be something as heartbreaking as a serious illness or your parents getting a divorce. Whatever trouble you face, God wants you to call on Him. In fact, He commands it.

God is not obligated to answer every prayer the way we want Him to. But He is obligated to keep His promises. Here, He promises to rescue you. The rescue may not look the way you want it to look. It may be better than you hoped for! In exchange for His promise to always rescue us, He wants us to honor Him, love Him with all our hearts, and tell others how great He is.

I need to be rescued, Father.
Thank You for always taking care of me.

Day 24

Speak of What Others Have Done for You

"But when all goes well with you, remember me and show me kindness; mention me to Pharaoh and get me out of this prison."
GENESIS 40:14 NIV

Have you read the story of Joseph in the Bible? After being sold into slavery by his brothers, he was falsely accused of a crime and thrown into prison. While there, Joseph helped interpret the dreams of two prisoners, a cupbearer and a baker, who both worked for Pharaoh. (Pharaoh was the Egyptian ruler.)

Pharaoh put the baker to death but restored the cupbearer to his position. Unfortunately, the cupbearer forgot to mention Joseph to Pharaoh, and Joseph stayed in prison for two more years.

It's important to remember what others have done for us and to speak of their gifts to others, especially if doing so helps them out. The stakes may not be as high as getting someone out of wrongful imprisonment, but the simple act of remembering shows incredible kindness.

Dear Jesus, sometimes I forget what others have done for me. Help me to remember other people and to do what I can to help them out in both my words and actions.

Day 25

The Fruit of the Holy Spirit

The Holy Spirit produces this kind of fruit in our lives: love, joy, peace, patience, kindness, goodness, faithfulness, gentleness, and self-control.
GALATIANS 5:22–23 NLT

When you choose Jesus and thus the Holy Spirit, you can start living the very best kind of life—life filled with good fruit! Not from the bowl on your counter or the produce section at the grocery store but the good fruit that God's Word describes. More love, joy, peace, patience, kindness, goodness, faithfulness, gentleness, and self-control in your mind, heart, and actions are all evidence that the Holy Spirit is living in you and making you increasingly like Jesus every day! What are the ways you can sense and see this fruit filling your life, and how are you sharing it with others?

Jesus, I praise You for the Holy Spirit filling me and producing good fruit in my life. Thank You for making me a better person each and every day as I grow more and more in my relationship with You. I pray others see the difference that You make in my life and want to trust in You as Savior and live for You too! Amen.

Day 26

Unchanging

"I am the Lord*, and I do not change."*
Malachi 3:6 nlt

Change is part of our lives—and that fact won't change. From major world events to the stuff going on for each of us individually, change is a constant. Think about your own life: Friends come and go, and your friend group tends to change from year to year. Maybe you changed schools or switched to homeschool. Maybe you changed churches or your parents had to change jobs. No matter how you slice it, life has a way of looking different, sometimes overnight!

You know what's *not* different? God. "Jesus Christ is the same yesterday and today and forever" (Hebrews 13:8 niv). He is the constant in the changing chaos. When you need a steady presence, a faithful friend, or unwavering advice, turn to Jesus. Choose to put your confidence in the unchanging nature of our reliable and trustworthy God!

Lord, all the constant change can make the world feel like it's spinning in chaos. Thank You for Your steady presence that centers me and calms me and guides me.

Day 27

Fear Not

"Do not fear, for I am with you. Do not be afraid, for I am your God. I will give you strength, and for sure I will help you. Yes, I will hold you up with My right hand that is right and good."

ISAIAH 41:10 NLV

Most of us struggle with fear and anxiety sometimes. Whether we're moving to a new neighborhood, prepping for a big test, or something else, fear is a normal human emotion. But many times in God's Word, He tells us not to fear. We are His children. He loves us. He is all-powerful, and He'll do whatever it takes to take care of us. He even sent His only Son to die in our place, because He knew we couldn't rescue ourselves.

But He doesn't stop at rescuing us. He helps us accomplish what we need to accomplish. He gives us strength and fortifies our abilities so we can be our best. When we think we can't, He says, "Yes, you can." He stands behind us and holds us up. There's no need to fear.

Thank You for holding me up. I trust You completely.

Day 28

Jesus Teaches Us How to Pray, Part 1

[Jesus] said to them, "When you pray, say: 'Father, hallowed be your name. Your kingdom come. Give us each day our daily bread, and forgive us our sins, for we ourselves forgive everyone who is indebted to us. And lead us not into temptation.'"

LUKE 11:2–4 ESV

Praying doesn't come easily sometimes, especially if you're just starting out in your relationship with God through Jesus Christ. It might feel really awkward. But Jesus gave us a clear, straightforward example of how to pray. First, we should spend time praising God and His holy name. We should ask for His kingdom to come, His will to be done. We should ask for our daily needs to be met. We should ask for forgiveness of our sins plus help and reminders to forgive others who sin against us. And we should ask for protection against temptation and sin. Is this the only way to pray? No, but it's Jesus' specific example, and we can let it guide us every moment as we talk to God.

Jesus, please keep bringing me back to Your teaching about prayer to guide me in good communication with You. Amen.

Day 29

Jesus Teaches Us How to Pray, Part 2

[Jesus said:] "Suppose you went to a friend's house at midnight, wanting to borrow three loaves of bread. You say to him, 'A friend of mine has just arrived for a visit, and I have nothing for him to eat.' And suppose he calls out from his bedroom, 'Don't bother me. . . .' But I tell you this—though he won't do it for friendship's sake, if you keep knocking long enough, he will get up and give you whatever you need because of your shameless persistence. And so I tell you, keep on asking, and you will receive what you ask for. Keep on seeking, and you will find. Keep on knocking, and the door will be opened to you."

LUKE 11:5–9 NLT

Jesus taught us to be persistent in prayer, so keep at it! As long as our requests don't go against His ways and His will, He hears us and wants to bless us with them. And if you're not sure if what you're asking Him goes against His ways and His will, keep reading His Word and asking Him to show you.

Jesus, I will keep on praying to You! Thank You! Amen.

Day 30

Jesus Teaches Us How to Pray, Part 3

[Jesus said:] "Would any of you fathers give your son a stone if he asked for bread? Or would you give a snake if he asked for a fish? Or if he asked for an egg, would you give him a small animal with a sting of poison? You are sinful and you know how to give good things to your children. How much more will your Father in heaven give the Holy Spirit to those who ask Him?"

LUKE 11:11–13 NLV

Jesus continued to teach about prayer in this way: If human dads who love their kids want to give them good gifts, how much more would our Creator, who is the one and only perfect loving Father, want to give us good gifts when we ask Him? If you believe in Jesus as the Savior who paid the price for your sin, you are in close relationship with your heavenly Father. And His Word promises He wants to bless you with the very best kind of gifts—and those best gifts are found through the Holy Spirit working in your life.

Jesus, thank You for teaching me about prayer and good gifts. Amen.

Day 31

Confess Your Sins to Each Other

Make this your common practice: Confess your sins to each other and pray for each other so that you can live together whole and healed.

James 5:16 MSG

Have you ever done something wrong and thought, *Well, nobody saw what I did, so I can just keep it to myself and no one will ever know!*

God doesn't want us to shove our sin into a drawer and forget about it. Keeping sin in the dark brings guilt, shame, and sometimes even more sin.

Confessing your sins both to God and to others brings healing and spiritual freedom. In fact, sharing your struggles and victories can uniquely encourage other believers. By sharing your story, you could help bring wholeness and healing to others.

Lord Jesus, confessing my sins is scary. What if people judge me or make fun of me? Give me the courage to confess my struggles to those who will understand, and help me conquer my sin.

Day 32

God Is Good

The Lord is good and does what is right;
he shows the proper path to those who go astray.
Psalm 25:8 NLT

The very nature of God is *good.* He is the ultimate standard of excellence, virtue, moral uprightness, and worthiness. "Taste and see that the Lord is good," said the psalmist. "Oh, the joys of those who take refuge in him!" (Psalm 34:8 NLT). The Bible testifies many times to the goodness of the Lord (2 Chronicles 5:13; Psalm 100:5; 106:1; Nahum 1:7).

Satan likes to sneakily whisper that God is *not* good: He can't be trusted. He's a stern judge or an abusive, absent Father who doesn't really care about you. Satan will use the failings of earthly fathers or other adults to distort our perception of God. We must recognize these lies and allow the truth to rehabilitate our view of God.

How are you tempted to believe God isn't good? Ask God to help you have confidence in His goodness.

Lord, help me taste and see that You are good. Correct my perception of You so I can understand who You really are.

Day 33

Strong and Courageous

"Have I not commanded you? Be strong and courageous. Do not be afraid; do not be discouraged, for the LORD your God will be with you wherever you go."

JOSHUA 1:9 NIV

Did you know fear is the opposite of hope? Fear is the belief that something bad will happen, and hope is the belief that something good will happen. God tells us to be strong and courageous because we are His children. He tells us not to be afraid because He is on our side. With Him, we have the promise of good things. That doesn't mean we won't ever face scary things. But we can have courage in the face of those frightening events, knowing God is with us, He will never leave us, and He has already set us up for victory.

Teach me to be strong and courageous, Father. I know that whatever I face, I face it with You beside me. Thank You for setting me up for victory.

Day 34

Forgive as Christ Forgave You

Bear with each other and forgive one another if any of you has a grievance against someone. Forgive as the Lord forgave you.

Colossians 3:13 NIV

Conflicts happen, even among Christians. Sometimes it stings worse when a Christian friend hurts us because we often hold those following Jesus to a higher standard. We must choose to let things go, to forgive, and to be gentle toward fellow believers who hurt or offend us.

If you're struggling to forgive someone today, think about how God forgave you: freely, fully, and before you even knew you'd sinned. If a brother or sister in Christ hurts you, forgive quickly and trust that the Holy Spirit is working on their heart, just like He's working on yours.

Why is forgiveness so hard, God? Help me let go of the anger and hurt I feel, especially toward people who share my faith in You.

Day 35

New Wardrobe

So, chosen by God for this new life of love, dress in the wardrobe God picked out for you: compassion, kindness, humility, quiet strength, discipline.

COLOSSIANS 3:12 MSG

Have you ever considered there's a wardrobe change of sorts once you accept Jesus as your personal Savior, believing Him to be God's one and only Son? When you become a believer, there is a supernatural change that happens. It's a change of heart that manifests as a change of behavior. And it's wonderful.

Where you used to be snarky and selfish, you're now more compassionate. Kindness comes out more often than harsh responses. There's a humility that makes you approachable. And rather than react in hurtful ways, you're able to take a breath and be loving. Your relationship with God changes everything. And it's only through His power and grace that this kind of change is possible.

Lord, thank You for my new wardrobe of compassion, kindness, humility, and strength. Help me choose to walk throughout my day proudly wearing it. Let every word and action reflect the changes You've made in my life.

Day 36

He Is with You

The word of the L*ORD came to me, saying, "Before I formed you in the womb I knew you, before you were born I set you apart. . ." "Alas, Sovereign* L*ORD," I said, "I do not know how to speak; I am too young." But the* L*ORD said to me, "Do not say, 'I am too young.' You must go to everyone I send you to and say whatever I command you. Do not be afraid of them, for I am with you and will rescue you."*

JEREMIAH 1:4–8 NIV

Before you existed, the Lord knew you. He formed you just the way you are and planned your life. When you feel nervous about the things He asks you to do, tell Him about your hesitation. Admit when you're afraid. Instead of feeling stuck in your fear, ask Him to help. Ask for His strength. Ask Him to work through you. You don't have to be afraid, because He's with you. He will rescue you.

Lord, I'm so glad You're with me.
I want to trust You and not live in fear.

Day 37

Mercy!

Answer me when I pray to you, my God who does what is right. Make things easier for me when I am in trouble. Have mercy on me and hear my prayer.

PSALM 4:1 NCV

In the middle of all the troubles of life, God can be trusted as one who does what is right. Because He is good and because He hears and answers prayers, it's vital to remember to pray to Him. Don't try to do things all on your own, whether in your own power or your own understanding. Ask for His help! Ask for Him to work and do what is right in your life. When you feel like life is especially difficult, ask God to make things easier for you. And when you're facing trouble after trouble, ask for His mercy.

God, You always do what is right. Please help me! I pray for Your mercy as I'm in trouble. Please hear my prayers and make things easier for me.

Day 38

Scripture Keeps Us Close to Jesus

You have been taught the holy Scriptures from childhood, and they have given you the wisdom to receive the salvation that comes by trusting in Christ Jesus. All Scripture is inspired by God and is useful to teach us what is true and to make us realize what is wrong in our lives. It corrects us when we are wrong and teaches us to do what is right. God uses it to prepare and equip his people to do every good work.

2 TIMOTHY 3:15–17 NLT

We can keep in close relationship with Jesus by constantly learning from His Word. We can trust that every bit of the Bible is inspired by God. With His Word, He corrects us, prepares us, and equips us for every good thing He has planned for us. We should regularly spend time reading the Bible and praying like this:

> Jesus, through scripture today, please teach me more about You and how You want me to live. Please give me wisdom, knowledge, and more understanding. Encourage me and show me Your awesome love, protection, and care. Amen.

Day 39

Have You Asked?

Jabez cried out to the God of Israel, "Oh, that you would bless me and enlarge my territory! Let your hand be with me, and keep me from harm so that I will be free from pain." And God granted his request.

1 Chronicles 4:10 NIV

Jabez wasn't shy about asking God for success and blessings. Boldly, he asked the Lord to enlarge his territory and to keep him from harm. He asked for God's hand to be with him and to keep him free from pain. And what was God's response? He granted the request of Jabez.

God is free to answer your request in any way He chooses, yet Jabez left a great example to not be afraid to ask for God's favor. Instead of thinking you don't deserve God's good gifts, ask for His protection and blessing.

Father, please bless me! Enlarge my territory. Let Your hand be with me. And please, Lord, keep me from harm so that I will be free from pain.

Day 40

When I'm Afraid

When I am afraid, I put my trust in you.
PSALM 56:3 NIV

What kinds of things are you afraid of? Maybe you freak out at the thought of giving a report in front of your class. Or maybe lightning and thunder keep you awake at night. It could be that a scary movie or book gets your heart thumping in fear, or maybe you're terrified of meeting new people. God gives us a blank check when it comes to fear. Whatever it is that frightens us, we can run to Him. Call out to Him, and He's right there giving you courage, peace, and confidence. He is all-powerful, and you are His daughter. You don't ever have to feel afraid. . .but when you do, give it to Him. He will take care of you.

Thank You for understanding when I feel afraid. I'm so grateful that I can always come to You, no matter what, and You'll take care of me.

Day 41

Bear Each Other's Burdens

Bear one another's burdens, and so fulfill the law of Christ.
GALATIANS 6:2 ESV

Sometimes bearing a burden means taking care of someone's physical needs, such as babysitting, helping with household chores, or bringing meals. Other times, it means showing up during a difficult time, even when you don't know what to say or do.

When a burden involves death or disease, people often steer clear because they're afraid of saying or doing the wrong thing. It's incredibly kind to brave the awkwardness that comes with difficult situations and say, "I don't know what to say, but I'm so sorry. I'm here and I want to help."

We might not be able to fix someone's situation, but we can help keep it from crushing them by being present.

Dear Lord, help me be there for people when they're hurting. Give me the wisdom to know what to say and do so I can shoulder the burdens of those around me.

Day 42

I Need Help!

Help me, Lord my God; save me according to your unfailing love.
Psalm 109:26 NIV

Many people don't like asking for help. If you can figure out a way to make something happen or do it all by yourself, it can feel very satisfying to do the work all on your own.

Yet you were not created to live all alone. You're not expected to do absolutely everything all by yourself. God created you to be part of a bigger community—that's a very good reason He created families. Aside from the family and friends in your own life who would love to help you, you're never alone. God is there! When you know you can't do things all by yourself, ask Him for His help.

When you ask for His help, know that no request is too big for Him. His love never fails and it never ends. He will help you and save you.

Lord my God, please help me! I know Your love never ends. Please save me!

Day 43

The Command to Forgive

Be even-tempered, content with second place, quick to forgive an offense. Forgive as quickly and completely as the Master forgave you.
Colossians 3:13 MSG

One of the hardest ways we're told to love others is by forgiving them. We can be kind in the moment. We're able to smile or hug for a second or two. But sometimes, the thought of extending grace to someone who's deeply hurt us feels close to impossible. We don't want to let them off the hook for the pain they've caused. We don't want them to avoid the natural consequences of their actions. So we hold on to the offense.

Friend, this is a struggle we all face. Forgiving is hard, no matter how you slice it. But God commands it of His followers. He wants us to choose love over holding a grudge. Compassion over getting even. And when you can't seem to bring yourself to forgive, ask God to change your heart.

Lord, I want to be quick to forgive so nothing keeps me from choosing love. Fill me with grace for my friends and family. Amen.

Day 44

The Two Greatest Commandments

"Teacher, what is the most important commandment in the Law?" Jesus answered: Love the Lord your God with all your heart, soul, and mind. This is the first and most important commandment. The second most important commandment is like this one. And it is, "Love others as much as you love yourself."

MATTHEW 22:36–39 CEV

Jesus said the two most important commandments to obey are to love God first with all your heart, soul, and mind and to love your neighbor as yourself. If you focus on obeying these commandments, you will automatically do other things well too. Sometimes you'll hear people say something like "Jesus just says to love everyone. That's all you have to do." But they ignore the fact that Jesus said we are to love God first and most of all. We can't love others in the best ways that God intended unless we first love God with all our heart, soul, and mind—and that includes getting to know Him through His Word and through prayer.

Jesus, above everything else in my life, I want to obey these greatest commandments You taught. Please help me to stay focused. Amen.

Day 45

Always Present

"Be sure of this: I am with you always, even to the end of the age."
Matthew 28:20 NLT

Jesus never leaves your side. Ever! He's *always* with you—when you're walking the halls at school, competing in an event, navigating fickle relationships, or feeling lonely and left out. He *sees* you (Genesis 16:13). He *knows* you (Psalm 139:1–4). You cannot hide from Him (Psalm 139:7–10). He's the ultimate best friend.

Don't let your feelings make you doubt the truth. We don't always *feel* like God is listening, that He cares, or that He's near. When those doubts seep in, kick those lies to the curb and repeat what you know is true! You can be confident that God is with you right here, right now. And He's staying with you until He comes back to take you to be with Him forever. That's a promise!

Jesus, thank You for never leaving me! Even when I feel alone, I'm not. Help me remember that. Thank You for never letting me face scary or hard things by myself. Your faithful presence brings so much comfort.

Day 46

Talk to Him

Do not be anxious about anything, but in every situation, by prayer and petition, with thanksgiving, present your requests to God. And the peace of God, which transcends all understanding, will guard your hearts and your minds in Christ Jesus.

PHILIPPIANS 4:6–7 NIV

This verse tells us not to be anxious about anything. That doesn't mean we won't feel anxiety sometimes, but we're not supposed to live in that anxiety. As soon as we acknowledge that uneasy, scared, knotted-up feeling, we're supposed to talk to God about it. It doesn't matter what it is! If we're afraid because of something we can't control, or if we're freaked out because we messed up and we know we're in trouble. . .whatever it is, talk to God about it. He will gladly exchange your anxiety for His peace.

You know what's going on in my head right now, Father. You know I'm feeling anxious about ___. I believe You will handle this situation in a way that works out for my good. I love You, and I trust You.

Day 47

No One Beneath You

Live in harmony with one another. Do not be proud, but be willing to associate with people of low position. Do not be conceited.
ROMANS 12:16 NIV

If you look around a high school cafeteria, you can quickly see where everyone fits in. Musicians sit with their friends from orchestra, athletes sit with other athletes, and the popular kids all clump together in their cliques.

But what about those who don't belong to a certain table? Think of the hurt and pain when you aren't considered "good enough" to sit with a particular group.

Everyone wants popularity, friends, and to sit at the "cool" table. These are completely normal desires. However, we must be quick to include people who don't have a place to sit. Jesus extended friendship to the lowest members of society. Each day brings the opportunity to follow His example and include those the world wants to leave out.

Father God, help me see those who need a friend. Give me boldness to approach them and invite them to my table.

Day 48

Putting On Love

And regardless of what else you put on, wear love.
It's your basic, all-purpose garment. Never be without it.
Colossians 3:14 msg

Sometimes to change a behavior, muster courage, or find focus, it helps us to have a visual. Before a free throw in basketball, some people see the ball swish the net before they shoot. Before the hard conversation with a teacher, some will visualize a successful result in their mind first. Maybe you've done the same in your life at times. Choosing to love is no different.

What if before your feet hit the ground in the morning, you imagine putting on love like an oversized coat? It engulfs your body in abundance. Then as you go through your day and face challenging people, you can choose to love because there's so much to give. In those moments when you're faced with being kind or being dismissive, the decision is easier to make. In God's eyes, choosing love matters greatly!

Lord, I understand the value of wearing love. Help me put it on each day so I can treat others with kindness and compassion. Amen.

Day 49

Jesus Throughout the Bible

He took up our pain and bore our suffering. . . . He was pierced for our transgressions, he was crushed for our iniquities; the punishment that brought us peace was on him, and by his wounds we are healed.

ISAIAH 53:4–5 NIV

Jesus wasn't physically born into the world yet in the Old Testament of the Bible, but He is present throughout the Old Testament in the ways He is prophesied about and in other specific ways too. (See Luke 24:25–27; Acts 26:22–23; 1 Peter 1:10–12.) Isaiah 53 describes how He would take on our pain and suffering and the punishment for sin and be wounded in order to heal and save us from sin. And all of that was fulfilled through His death on the cross and resurrection.

Jesus, when I'm reading any book of the Bible, please help me see and understand how it all points toward You as the one and only hope of the world, the one and only Savior from sin. Amen.

Day 50

Creator

You alone are the Lord*, Creator of the heavens and all the stars, Creator of the earth and those who live on it, Creator of the ocean and all its creatures. You are the source of life, praised by the stars that fill the heavens.*

Nehemiah 9:6 CEV

God existed before all creation (Genesis 1:1). God made the world simply by speaking it into existence (Psalm 33:6, 9). As Creator, God fully controls all creation (Daniel 2:21; Luke 8:24). There's a lot of buzz about the dangers of climate change, but the destruction of the planet will not take place until its appointed time (Revelation 6). We are to be good stewards of the earth and care for it (Genesis 1:28), but God ultimately controls the earth's destiny. We can rest in confidence that He is Lord of all creation, the source of all life, and He will protect and preserve it until He builds the new heaven and new earth (Revelation 21:1).

I praise You, Creator God, for all that You've made. Help me care for Your creation yet relax with peace that You are in full control of the earth.

Day 51

Daughter of God

For the Spirit God gave us does not make us timid, but gives us power, love and self-discipline.
2 Timothy 1:7 NIV

Do you struggle with being timid and shy? Maybe you're outgoing in some situations, but other times you feel nervous. God wants you to remember you're His daughter. He has grafted you into His family, and His Spirit lives in you. He is almighty and all-powerful. There is nothing about Him that is timid or afraid of anything. . .and you have a family resemblance. You're royal! And who ever heard of a timid royal? Next time you feel nervous or afraid, hold your head high, look people in the eye, and remind yourself that you are God's powerful, loving, and confident daughter.

Thank You for this reminder that when I feel timid, anxious, or afraid, that doesn't come from You. You made me powerful and strong. You give me the ability to love when love is hard and to stand up for what's right when backing down is easier. Thank You for making me Your daughter.

Day 52

Supporting Friends

"I demand that you love each other as much as I love you. And here is how to measure it—the greatest love is shown when a person lays down his life for his friends."

JOHN 15:12–13 TLB

What are some ways you can support your friends sacrificially? Maybe you help them work through a tough class in school. Maybe you help them navigate a difficult situation at home. Maybe you help meet their basic needs by sharing your resources or connecting them with someone who can intervene. Or maybe you stand up for them, advocating when they feel weak or overwhelmed. By doing so, you are choosing love.

Ask God to open your eyes to the needs of those around you, because sometimes they are hard to see. Life gets busy. You have your own struggles to manage. And rather than see what others may need, we get focused on ourselves instead.

Lord, I care for my friends, and I don't want to be self-absorbed when they need my help. Let me be aware and sensitive to them, ready to love big at a moment's notice. Amen.

Day 53

Lay Down Your Life

"Greater love has no one than this, that someone lay down his life for his friends."
John 15:13 ESV

Jesus set the bar incredibly high when it came to loving others. He loved us so much that He willingly died on the cross so we could be cleansed of our sins.

Jesus also laid down His life while living, putting aside His own comfort to follow God and serve others. You may never be asked to die for your friends, but you can still lay down your life for them by following Jesus' example in living.

Think about what you could surrender in order to love others better. You could lay down your time, forgoing video games and Netflix binges to volunteer somewhere. You could lay down your comfort to bring Christ to unreached people. Or maybe you can lay down your plans for the day in order to be present for a friend in need.

Dear God, open my eyes to ways I can lay down my life for my friends. Reveal to me the selfishness in my life, and help me put my own desires aside to love others.

Day 54

Confession Time

I cried out to him for help, praising him as I spoke. If I had not confessed the sin in my heart, the Lord would not have listened. But God did listen! He paid attention to my prayer.

Psalm 66:17–19 NLT

The Lord is all-knowing and hears our thoughts and prayers—every single one. But if we truly want Him to listen and answer us, we must regularly admit our sins, not hold on to them (or cherish them as some versions of this scripture put it). The Bible promises that God forgives us and removes our sin as far as the east is from the west (Psalm 103:12), but first we must confess those sins. That keeps us humble and depending on Jesus and His saving grace, which is the very best blessing—to be dependent on the one who loved (and continues to love) us so much He was willing to die for us.

Jesus, You know I make many mistakes, and I don't want to hide them or pretend like I don't sin. These are my sins I've been struggling with: ________. Please forgive me for them and remove them from me. Thank You! Amen.

Day 55

Silent Testimony

For ever since the world was created, people have seen the earth and sky. Through everything God made, they can clearly see his invisible qualities—his eternal power and divine nature. So they have no excuse for not knowing God.

Romans 1:20 NLT

All of creation clearly reveals the nature and character of God. "The heavens proclaim the glory of God. The skies display his craftsmanship. Day after day they continue to speak; night after night they make him known. They speak without a sound or word; their voice is never heard. Yet their message has gone throughout the earth, and their words to all the world" (Psalm 19:1–4 NLT).

The delicate bloom of a flower speaks of God's love for beauty and creativity. A garden bursting with vegetables proclaims God's ability to bring life from death: dead seeds planted in the ground transform into living, fruit-bearing plants.

Look outside. What do you see? What does it reveal to you about God?

God, how amazing that all of creation speaks of You without saying a word! Help me stop and notice. Help me have a deeper understanding of You through observing Your handiwork around me.

Day 56

Stop Grumbling

Do everything without grumbling or arguing.
Philippians 2:14 NIV

This is one of those hard verses. It's one thing to generally have a good attitude. . .but this doesn't say to do *most* things with a pleasant spirit. That word *everything* is all-inclusive. It means Every. Little. Thing. We're not supposed to grumble or argue, ever. Why would God make us do something so hard?

God knows grumbling is pointless. So is arguing. If we have a problem with someone or with the way something is handled, we should go to the person and speak to them humbly, with love. We should try to see their side of things. And if we still must do the thing we don't want to do, it's a whole lot more pleasant to just do it without comment. Next time you feel like grumbling or arguing, ask God to change your heart, give you a sweet spirit, and help you to move forward with love.

Help me do all things with Your love.
I want to shine Your spirit in all circumstances.

Day 57

Take Jesus at His Word

Jesus told him, "Go back home. Your son will live!"
John 4:50 NLT

The government official in the story in John 4 had legal authority over Jesus, but he respected Jesus. He came to Jesus and begged Him to heal his son who was sick. And Jesus said, "Go back home. Your son will live!" With his authority, the official could have ordered Jesus to come to his son in person to heal him. But the official decided to believe Jesus had the miraculous power to heal from anywhere, even from afar, and he trusted Jesus would do it. He took Jesus at His word and headed home.

While the official was still traveling, some of his servants met him along the way and told him his son was well again. The official asked, "What time did he get better?" When his servants named the time, the official realized that was the exact time that Jesus had said to him, "Your son will live." From then on, not only did the official believe in Jesus but so did everyone in his household.

Jesus, I choose to take You at Your word. Amen.

Day 58

Speaking Without Fear

"And now, Lord, listen to their threats. Lord, help us, your servants, to speak your word without fear. Show us your power to heal. Give proofs and make miracles happen by the power of Jesus, your holy servant."

Acts 4:29–30 NCV

After Jesus died, rose from the dead, and went to heaven, His disciples faced a lot of trouble from Jewish leaders. In fact, many nonbelievers threatened members of the early church. Peter, John, and their friends didn't know what to do about the threats. But they knew they needed to tell everyone about Jesus. When they faced danger and opposition, the best thing the disciples did was pray for God to step in and work. They asked for God's help and power.

Just like the early disciples, when you face danger and opposition, pray! Ask God for His help. Ask Him to keep you from being afraid. And ask Him to make miracles happen. You don't have to face your troubles alone!

Lord, please help me! I want to speak Your Word without fear. Make miracles happen and help me do it.

Day 59

Slow to Anger

The Lord *passed in front of Moses, calling out, "Yahweh! The* Lord*! The God of compassion and mercy! I am slow to anger and filled with unfailing love and faithfulness."*
Exodus 34:6 NLT

Satan loves to distort our view of God. One of his tactics is to make us believe God is an angry judge who sits in heaven and frowns at us all the time. You might laugh, but how easily do you believe these lies? "God is punishing me." "God is disappointed in me." "God is frustrated with me."

Because God is pictured as a Father, Satan also loves to mold your view of God the Father to match the imperfect example of your earthly father. If your earthly father abandoned you, abused you, or is quick to be angry at you, you may believe God the Father is like that too. But let the truth sink in: God is a God of compassion and mercy. He is *slow to anger* and filled with *unfailing* love and faithfulness!

Yahweh, reveal the lies I believe about Your character, and help me remain confident that You always view me with compassion and love.

Day 60

Silly Fights

Don't have anything to do with foolish and stupid arguments, because you know they produce quarrels. And the Lord's servant must not be quarrelsome but must be kind to everyone, able to teach, not resentful.

2 Timothy 2:23–24 NIV

Have you ever watched two people in a stupid, foolish argument? Usually, it's about something nobody really cares about anyway. The argument is really about pride, and neither person wants to back down. It would be so much more pleasant for everyone involved if one person said, "That's okay. You can win this one. It doesn't really matter anyway."

When we refuse to back down from a silly argument, we're really saying we think we're more important than the other person. Christ had a humble attitude when He was on earth, always putting others first. That's how He wants us to act too. When we act humbly, we avoid these silly quarrels. We make others feel loved and important, and Christ's light shines through us.

Help me avoid silly arguments. Teach me to be humble, Lord.

Day 61

Protected

Do not withhold your mercy from me, LORD*;*
may your love and faithfulness always protect me.
PSALM 40:11 NIV

When you face difficulties and tough situations in life, sometimes you might feel like it's more than you can handle. Enough is enough. You just want all your challenges and trials to stop!

Cry out to the Lord for His mercy. Honestly tell Him that you can't carry this heavy weight anymore. You need His faithful love and compassion. You need His help!

After you've begged for His mercy, ask for His protection too. Not only can He protect you physically, but He'll also protect you mentally, emotionally, and spiritually. All of this protection is just a part of His love and His faithfulness.

Lord, it's such a relief to know that Your love and faithfulness will always keep me safe! Thank You for Your mercy and protection!

Day 62

Keep Your Eyes Forward

Make it your goal to live a quiet life, minding your own business and working with your hands, just as we instructed you before.

1 Thessalonians 4:11 NLT

There are many times when it's right and good to step in and help someone in need. Sometimes though, the kindest and wisest thing you can do is mind your own business and keep living your life peacefully.

For example, if you hear a piece of gossip floating around, don't become curious and try to find out more. Before long, instead of "helping" the situation, you'll actually start contributing to the problem.

Instead, step away from gossip. Unless you're in a position to say something that stops it, don't feed the flames of slander and meanness. Instead, walk away and go do something productive and meaningful with your time.

Dear God, I'm sorry for the times I've gotten involved in things that were none of my business. Help me walk away from gossip and spend my time wisely.

Day 63

Our One and Only Savior

Jesus is holy and has no guilt. He has never sinned and is different from sinful men. He has the place of honor above the heavens. Christ is not like other religious leaders. They had to give gifts every day on the altar in worship for their own sins first and then for the sins of the people. Christ did not have to do that. He gave one gift on the altar and that gift was Himself. It was done once and it was for all time.

HEBREWS 7:26–27 NLV

Have you ever heard people say that all religions are the same? If you spend even a small amount of time learning about other religions, you realize it's just not true. Belief in Jesus as God and as our one and only Savior is the one true religion. Jesus alone was (and is) perfect and holy and without sin. He gave His own life once for all people of all time, and no other religion offers that kind of gift and love and miracle!

Jesus, there is truly no one else like You! You are God, and You are the one true Savior! Thank You for giving Your life to save everyone who believes in You! Amen.

Day 64

God of Mercy

"I am merciful."
Exodus 22:27 NLT

Theologians (a.k.a. really smart people) often define mercy as not getting what we deserve. We all sin, and everyone falls short of God's perfect standard (Romans 3:23). The punishment for our sin is death (Romans 6:23). Period. That's what we deserve. But God, in His incredible love, sent His Son to take our place (John 3:16). Jesus came to earth, lived a perfect life, and died on the cross—taking the punishment of death for us.

We've all had moments when we messed up big-time. We waited anxiously for the punishment we knew we deserved—and received mercy instead. That's just a small taste of the mercy God shows us. You can be certain God is not holding your sins against you or waiting to punish you for every failure. Yeah, you sin and mess up. But when you come to Him for forgiveness, He says, "I am merciful. You are forgiven." So live in freedom from guilt and with gratefulness for the amazing gift of mercy!

Merciful God, thank You for not giving me what I deserve! Help me show mercy to others in return.

Day 65

Expectations

To be obedient, to be ready to do whatever is good, to slander no one, to be peaceable and considerate, and always to be gentle toward everyone.

TITUS 3:1–2 NIV

According to social media, there's an exhausting list of things you're expected to be—funny, smart, beautiful, healthy, stylish. . . . There's nothing wrong with trying to be your best, but it's important to remember that God's goals for us look different than the world's expectations.

He wants us to be obedient first to Him then to our parents and those in authority over us. He wants us to be good, kind, and compassionate. He wants our words to build others up, not tear them down. Really, He wants us to *love.* Honestly, people care a lot less about how we look than about how we make them feel. When we love others well—the way God loves them—they view us as one of their favorite people. Even more importantly, God will be pleased, and we'll be blessed.

Teach me the proper balance, Lord. I want to value Your expectations more than the world's.

Day 66

Sadness

When I heard these things, I sat down and cried for several days. I was sad and fasted. I prayed to the God of heaven, "Lord, God of heaven, you are the great God who is to be respected. You are loyal, and you keep your agreement with those who love you and obey your commands."

Nehemiah 1:4–5 NCV

Unfortunately, bad news is part of life. You might hear something that breaks your heart or disappoints you. When you do hear bad news, it's okay to be sad about it. Cry. Don't feel like you need to be cheery or pretend like everything is all right. Spend some time in your grief and mourn.

Yet don't forget to include the Lord in your emotional response. Remember who He is and pray, even as your heart feels like it's breaking. Praise the Lord even in your sadness. Remember He is great. He is loyal. He should be respected. He keeps His promises to all who love and obey Him.

Lord God of heaven, You are the great and loyal God. I respect, love, and obey You.

Day 67

Encourage Good Works

And let's consider how to encourage one another in love and good deeds.

HEBREWS 10:24 NASB

Recently, a friend at my church shared with me how she got up the courage to tell one of her neighbors about Jesus. Her boldness to speak truth, even though it was uncomfortable at first, inspired me to look for more ways to share Christ. Her actions stirred me to good works.

You never know the impact an act of kindness or obedience has on those around you. Your gentle words might make someone stop and think about how they've been treating others. Your willingness to forgive someone who's wronged you might help someone let go of a grudge they've been carrying. Never pass up an opportunity to do good, for a single act of kindness may push back the darkness for ages to come.

Heavenly Father, make my words and actions stir others to do good works in Your name.

Day 68

Go to Church

We must hold tightly to the hope we say is ours. After all, we can trust the one who made the agreement with us. We should keep on encouraging each other to be thoughtful and to do helpful things. Some people have given up the habit of meeting for worship, but we must not do that. We should keep on encouraging each other, especially since you know that the day of the Lord's coming is getting closer.

HEBREWS 10:23–25 CEV

The Bible tells us that we need to meet together regularly with other Christians who choose to trust Jesus as their Savior too. We need to worship and learn more about God together; and we need to encourage, comfort, and take good care of each other!

> Jesus, thank You for all the other Christians who are in my life and for those all over the world! Help us to love getting together at church to grow closer to You and to each other. Amen.

Day 69

Lord Who Heals

"I am the Lord *who heals you."*
Exodus 15:26 NCV

"Dear Lord, please heal so-and-so who's sick. Help them feel better." How often have you prayed something like that? Probably a lot! There's nothing wrong with praying for physical healing—whether for small things like a cold or big things like cancer. But God heals in a much deeper way than just our physical ailments. He wants to heal us *fully*—emotionally, spiritually, and physically. He wants to heal your mind of all the lies you believe about yourself. He wants to heal your emotions and all the past wounds that keep causing you emotional pain. He wants to heal you spiritually—first through salvation by restoring your relationship with Him, then by healing all the misperceptions you have that keep you distant and distrustful of Him. Will you pray today and ask God for healing—true, deep healing—where you need it?

Lord, please heal me! I'm broken and hurting, and I need Your healing touch. Heal the lies with Your truth. Heal my brokenness with Your love.

Day 70

But Love Is the Greatest

Three things will last forever—faith, hope, and love—and the greatest of these is love.

1 Corinthians 13:13 NLT

Friend, what characterizes your life? How would people describe you? It matters to God because He is crystal clear on what should set you apart from unbelievers. And because it matters to Him, it should matter to us too.

Our *faith* should stand out in how we act and what we say. It ought to be obvious to others that we value following God's commands and trust His leading, even when it's hard to do. In addition, *hope* should define our attitude. When life gets messy, our outlook should be expectant as we trust God to show up. But most of all—more than anything else—*love* should be what characterizes us. In every relationship and in all circumstances, He wants us to lead with it. God wants you to choose love every time.

Lord, let faith, hope, and love be what defines my life. Help me reflect these to my friends and family every day. Amen.

Day 71

Frustrated by Wrong

For you are not a God who is pleased with wickedness; with you, evil people are not welcome. The arrogant cannot stand in your presence. You hate all who do wrong; you destroy those who tell lies. The bloodthirsty and deceitful you, Lord, detest.

Psalm 5:4–6 NIV

It's hard to live out your faith day after day when you see evil being celebrated in this world. But in Psalm 5, David shows that it's good to come to the Lord even when you're surrounded by bad.

When wickedness, evil, arrogance, lying, and wrong living upset you, tell the Lord about it! In prayer, tell Him what you see wrong with the world. He's not pleased with all the sin either. Yet He can and will do something about it. He detests what's wrong and will destroy evil.

Instead of bottling up all your frustration, anger, and disgust, tell God about it. Ask for Him to work. Ask for His help in navigating life right now. He'll hear your prayer and respond.

Lord, You are perfect! You are holy. I pray You would put an end to all the wickedness and evil around me.

Day 72

Triune God

In the beginning was the Word, and the Word was with God, and the Word was God. He was in the beginning with God. All things were made through him, and without him was not any thing made that was made. . . . And the Word became flesh and dwelt among us, and we have seen his glory, glory as of the only Son from the Father, full of grace and truth.

John 1:1–3, 14 ESV

Jesus has always existed and has always been God because God is triune, meaning existing in three—Father, Son, and Holy Spirit—who are distinct but equal. So we learn about Jesus throughout the whole Bible.

Jesus, as I read Your Word, show me all the great things I can learn about You throughout both Old Testament and New. I want to know You better and follow You every day. Amen.

Day 73

God Who Sees

She gave this name to the LORD who spoke to her: "You are the God who sees me," for she said, "I have now seen the One who sees me."
GENESIS 16:13 NIV

Hagar was fleeing a desperate situation. Her mistress Sarai, not confident in God's promises, gave Hagar to her husband, Abram, so Sarai could have children through Hagar. The plan worked. Hagar became pregnant, but Hagar despised Sarai for it. In return, Sarai abused her so much that Hagar ran away. She was pregnant, alone, and in the middle of a desert when the Lord appeared. What did He tell her? Go back to Sarai and submit to her (Genesis 16:9). *What?!* Hagar had been sorely used, but the Lord would not abandon her. He promised blessing.

Hagar's encounter with God proved that He saw her circumstances and cared about her. Their meeting gave her the confidence to go back to Sarai and submit. Hagar knew she was not abandoned and alone. The God Who Sees Me stood beside her.

God Who Sees Me, I know You care about me.
Give me confidence today as I face my own circumstances.

Day 74

Forgiven

For the sake of your name, Lord, forgive my many sins.
Psalm 25:11 NCV

Whether you call it messing up, making a mistake, doing what you know you shouldn't do, or sinning, you do wrong things every single day. Absolutely every person does. It's impossible to live a sinless, perfect life of innocence.

Even though everyone sins, it's not like you should celebrate your sin. And it's not like you're invited to keep sinning more because you feel like you can't help yourself.

When you know you've done something wrong, stop and apologize. First, apologize to the Lord, then apologize to anyone you've wronged. After you've apologized, ask for forgiveness. Once you ask God for forgiveness, it's time to change your ways. If you know you keep repeating your same sins over and over again, ask Him for help to change. Ask Him to help take your temptation away.

> Lord, I'm sorry that I've sinned against You. Please forgive me! Please help me move past my sins and stop giving in to temptation.

Day 75

The Command to Love

"Now I am giving you a new commandment: Love each other. Just as I have loved you, you should love each other."
JOHN 13:34 NLT

In His Word, God talks often about the command to love. It's not a mere suggestion but a deep desire for His followers. Because of the love lavished on us, we're to expend love on others with similar passion and purpose. How are you doing with that?

Are you showing love to your parents, even when they drive you nuts? Are you being kind to your siblings, giving them time and attention on the regular? When at school or on the court, are you respectful to your teachers and coaches? Do you show compassion to those who need a friend or advocate? Are you devoted to being thoughtful toward others—especially the ones who may not agree with you? At every chance, choose to love in ways that will bless others and glorify the Lord.

Lord, let my heart always be bent toward loving others deeply and fully. Amen.

Day 76

Learn to Love Kindness

He has told you, O man, what is good; and what does the Lord *require of you but to do justice, and to love kindness, and to walk humbly with your God?*

Micah 6:8 ESV

Take a moment and think about recent opportunities you've had to show kindness to others. Did you show kindness out of obligation or because other people were watching and you wanted to look good? Or did you extend kindness because you love being kind?

Sometimes the first step to *loving* something is *doing* it, even if the feelings aren't quite there yet. Maybe you already love kindness, or maybe you don't see the point. By trusting the Lord and obeying His command for kindness, you'll eventually fall in love with the joy that comes with doing good. Kindness will take root in your life, and the resulting fruit will bless everyone in your circle.

Dear Jesus, please give me a genuine love of kindness.

Day 77

You Are the Light

"You are the light of the world—like a city on a hilltop that cannot be hidden. No one lights a lamp and then puts it under a basket. Instead, a lamp is placed on a stand, where it gives light to everyone in the house. In the same way, let your good deeds shine out for all to see, so that everyone will praise your heavenly Father."

MATTHEW 5:14–16 NLT

The light of the world—that's a big deal! That's what Jesus has said about you and all believers when we trust Him as Savior. With the Holy Spirit living inside us, our job is to shine our lights that point to Him so that others will want to trust Jesus as Savior and praise God too! We should never want to conceal our light. So many people in the dark world around us need the good news and love of Jesus, so we need to shine as brightly as possible!

Jesus, it's incredible to be the light of the world because of You! I want to shine Your love brightly to everyone around me and give God all the praise! Amen.

Day 78

God Our Helper

God is our refuge and strength, always ready to help in times of trouble. So we will not fear when earthquakes come and the mountains crumble into the sea. Let the oceans roar and foam. Let the mountains tremble as the waters surge!
PSALM 46:1–3 NLT

Just watching news headlines for a single day shows a world falling apart. The fear and hysteria—this is a world without God. But we are not without God! He is our shelter, a place of protection we can rest under while storms rage. He is our strength; He gives courage amid all the fear. We don't have to be afraid, because He is always near, always ready to help us.

You do not face this day—or any day—alone. Keep your eyes firmly fixed on mighty God, not the world falling apart. God alone can give you confidence and peace. Let that confidence and peace fill you and shine through you.

> Lord, I run to You as my shelter and help. Give me strength and courage. May Your peace flow through me to reassure and encourage others.

Day 79

True Friends

Faithful are the wounds of a friend;
profuse are the kisses of an enemy.
PROVERBS 27:6 ESV

Have you ever had to tell a friend something for her own good, that you knew she didn't want to hear? Did you struggle with how to tell her because you care about her and didn't want to hurt her? When we don't really care about someone, we're fine with telling them whatever they want to hear. After all, why bother with the drama of making them angry?

But if we're truly concerned over someone's well-being, we'll tell them the hard truth. We'll do it privately, and we'll say it with love and encouragement. If someone only ever tells you nice things, you might question their sincerity. If they repeatedly say unkind things in a way that's hurtful and embarrassing, you might rethink the friendship. But a person who encourages you, supports you, and tells you hard things in a loving way. . .that's a friend you want to keep.

Bring me true friends, Lord.
And teach me to be this kind of friend.

Day 80

Questions?

After these things happened, the LORD *spoke his word to Abram in a vision: "Abram, don't be afraid. I will defend you, and I will give you a great reward." But Abram said, "Lord* GOD*, what can you give me? . . . Look, you have given me no son, so a slave born in my house will inherit everything I have."*

GENESIS 15:1–3 NCV

After God told Abram a great promise for his future, Abram didn't celebrate or even thank the Lord. He questioned God. Not understanding how the Lord would fulfill His promise, Abram was caught up in the details. Before accepting God's promise with belief, he wanted answers.

Abram became the father of many nations all through God's faithfulness and miraculous gifts. If Abram questioned God, don't feel embarrassed to ask God for clarification. Ask for understanding if you feel like you need it. The important thing is to come to your heavenly Father with honesty. Work through your questions with Him.

Father, please help me understand Your will for my life. Please help me trust You in faith!

Day 81

Actions Speak Louder

"Your love for one another will prove to the world that you are my disciples."

John 13:35 NLT

Actions matter more than words. You can tell someone you love them, but when the heat is turned up in their life, do you show them love? Do you reach out in support? Do you rally around them in compassion? Do you find ways to meet their immediate and pressing needs? Our words don't matter if our actions don't match them.

The Word says that people will know we love God by how we love others. The ways we treat those around us will reveal our faith. And the more time you spend deepening your relationship with the Lord through prayer, time in the Bible, and meditating on scripture, the more love will become your default response in life. When that happens, your actions will point to God in heaven. Choosing love reveals your heart for the Lord and following His ways.

Lord, help me live in such a way that my friends and family know I am a Christ follower. Let my actions and words of love align in wonderful ways. Amen.

Day 82

Jesus Often Taught in Parables

His disciples came and asked him, "Why do you use parables when you talk to the people?"

MATTHEW 13:10 NLT

Jesus answered this question: "This is why I speak to them in picture-stories. They have eyes but they do not see. They have ears but they do not hear and they do not understand. It happened in their lives as Isaiah said it would happen. He said, 'You hear and hear but do not understand. You look and look but do not see. . . . They hear very little with their ears. They have closed their eyes. If they did not do this, they would see with their eyes and hear with their ears and understand with their hearts. Then they would be changed in their ways, and I would heal them' " (Matthew 13:13–15 NLV).

Remember this answer from Jesus, and pray for understanding as you study His parables, His example, and all the writings in the Bible. We want to have eyes, ears, minds, and hearts that are open and paying attention so we understand how God is trying to teach us.

Jesus, please give me understanding as I read Your Word and learn from Your teaching. Amen.

Day 83

God Our Rescue

"I am the Lord *your God, who rescued you from the land of Egypt, the place of your slavery."*
Exodus 20:2 NLT

The Israelites lived as severely oppressed slaves to the pharaoh of Egypt. They lived in despair, depression, and bondage. They were stuck and had no way out—until God stepped in and rescued them.

We all have our own Egypts and places of slavery. How do you feel enslaved? What has a hold on you and makes you feel trapped and helpless? Are you a victim of bullying? Are you a slave to food and live in despair and depression about your weight? Are you a slave to popularity and can't make yourself leave the popular crowd? Are you a slave to fashion and beauty? A certain sport? An addiction? Call out to the Lord your God, who rescues you from the place of your slavery! He will free you and guide you out of your Egypt if you're willing to follow Him.

Lord, rescue me from my slavery! I can't do it on my own. Guide me out of this pit, and help me have the courage to follow You.

Day 84

Persecuted

"Blessed are you when people insult you and persecute you, and falsely say all kinds of evil against you because of Me."
MATTHEW 5:11 NASB

Most of us have been the victims of gossip and bullying at some point. If people say mean things about us, that's wrong. But if the things they say are directly related to our choice to live for Christ, there's a reward attached! If people make fun of you for doing the right thing, God sees. If others are cruel because you refuse to go along with the crowd when you know the crowd is wrong, God notices.

Being persecuted stinks. It never feels good in the moment. But hang in there. Keep doing the honorable thing. Keep being kind when others are cruel. Keep standing up for what's right when others are doing wrong. God will reward you. And when He does, it will be worth it.

> I don't want to be persecuted for serving You, Lord. But I will serve You no matter what. Help me stay strong.

Day 85

Use Your Gift to Serve Others

God has given each of you a gift from his great variety of spiritual gifts. Use them well to serve one another.

1 PETER 4:10 NLT

When God adopted you, He equipped you with a gift (or several!) to build up other believers. Your personality, patience with children, joy, sense of humor, eye for detail, ability to teach, artistic skills, knack for organization, or whatever else you possess was given to you by God to serve and expand His kingdom.

Think about the gifts you have to share with your church. No gift is too small or less important. If you're using what God gave you to serve Him, you're blessing your brothers and sisters in the Lord and bringing joy to the heart of God.

I want to use my talents to serve You, Lord. Reveal to me my gifts, and provide me with opportunities to use them for Your kingdom.

Day 86

Believing by Faith

Abram believed the Lord. *And the* Lord *accepted Abram's faith, and that faith made him right with God.*

Genesis 15:6 NCV

Just because Abram questioned the Lord's ability and plan, it didn't mean that he didn't believe the Lord. Ultimately, through his faith, Abram chose to believe that God could deliver on His great promises. And God did.

Just like Abram is praised for his faith and belief, you can be too. When you feel like you're plagued with doubt, ask God for understanding, then choose to step out in faith and believe. Watch the way God will fulfill His promises and be faithful in your life. Believe the Lord. Your faith will make you right with God.

Father God, I want to believe You! I want to step out in faith and do the unbelievable and seemingly impossible things You've called me to do. Please help me as I walk step-by-step with You.

Day 87

Dealing with Doubt

But Moses said to God, "I am not a great man! How can I go to the king and lead the Israelites out of Egypt?"
Exodus 3:11 NCV

When you read the story of Moses in Exodus, you'll discover that God asked him to do some pretty amazing, very gutsy, and ridiculously brave things. At first, Moses wasn't so sure. And he told God about his doubts and fears. But the Lord had other plans and proved time after time that He could use Moses in mighty ways.

God may have amazing plans for you and your life too. He can use you in mighty ways. When you feel like He's pushing you to do something that seems scary, tell Him your doubts and fears. Don't be afraid to admit that you're wondering why He's choosing you. You don't have to hide your feelings from the Lord.

Lord, You have so many truly wonderful things planned for those who love You. I love You! And I'm willing to do what You've planned for me, even if it's scary.

Day 88

Choose to Be a Child of God

See what great love the Father has lavished on us, that we should be called children of God! And that is what we are!

1 John 3:1 NIV

When we choose to trust in Jesus as Savior, we can have a close relationship with God as our heavenly Father. It's so wonderful to have earthly family but even better to know we are in the family of the one true almighty God. Sometimes troubles in earthly families get totally out of control. Earthly families can break apart. So being part of God's family is especially important because we know that no matter what goes on in earthly families, we are always God's children and *no one* can break that bond. With the one true almighty God as our loving Father, we have all His care and protection every single day of our lives.

Jesus, I'm so thankful that because of You, I'm a child of almighty God, who loves and takes good care of me now and forever. Amen.

Day 89

Mighty Defender

"So no weapon that is used against you will defeat you. You will show that those who speak against you are wrong. These are the good things my servants receive. Their victory comes from me," says the LORD.

ISAIAH 54:17 NCV

When you're on God's team, attacks *will* come. You can count on it. God has an enemy, and choosing God's side puts a target on your back too. But God doesn't leave us defenseless! Choosing God's side means you're also choosing God's protection. The benefits of being on His team include a Mighty Defender who will not allow the enemy's attacks to defeat you. The battle and victory don't depend on you—God's in charge!

When gossip and slander are aimed at you, pray before you quickly jump to your own defense. Let God guide you and fight for you. When you're accused unfairly, check your anger and turn to the Lord to vindicate you. It's not on you to fight your way out of attacks. Put your confidence in God and let Him battle to victory for you.

Lord, I put my trust in You.
Please fight for me today and give me wisdom.

Day 90

Judgy

"For in the way you judge, you will be judged; and by your standard of measure, it will be measured to you."
MATTHEW 7:2 NASB

It's easy to judge other people. Sometimes we don't even know we're doing it. We look at someone's choices or circumstances and think, "I'd never do that." The truth is, we don't know what someone else has gone through to lead them to this place. We don't know their deepest hurts or their toughest battles. Only God knows those things, and He offers them grace and forgiveness. He holds out His arms in love. Why shouldn't we do the same?

God is very clear about our job descriptions. Our job is to love. His job is to judge. If we judge others harshly, we're asking God to judge us harshly. If we show others compassion and grace, He'll treat us that way too. Let's be honest. We're not good at doing God's job for Him. Let's stick to our own task: to love, and let God judge others' actions.

Forgive me for judging those I disagree with and forgetting to show them love.

Day 91

Double-Checking

God said to Abram, "I am the LORD who led you out of Ur of Babylonia so that I could give you this land to own." But Abram said, "Lord GOD, how can I be sure that I will own this land?"

GENESIS 15:7–8 NCV

Even after Abram chose to believe the Lord through faith, he continued to question the Lord's ways. Abram asked the Lord for certainty.

God has a plan for you and your life. He knows exactly how He will work all things together for His good purposes. He will lead you where you need to go for His specific reasons. Yet He still welcomes your questions. Instead of barging ahead, thinking you know the exact thing He's planned for you to do, ask Him. Check along the way, and if you need certainty, ask Him for that. Keep walking by faith and keep communicating with your heavenly Father.

Thank You, Father, for the amazing plans You have for me. I pray You'll make things obvious for me. Show me the way I should go. Help me boldly and bravely follow You in faith. I want to live out Your purposes for my life.

Day 92

Let Go of Hatred

"You shall not hate your brother in your heart, but you shall reason frankly with your neighbor, lest you incur sin because of him."

Leviticus 19:17 ESV

When someone mistreats you, it's natural to be upset. Still, confronting people isn't fun. It would be much easier if the person who hurt you figured out what they did wrong and apologized on their own, right?

Most people want to avoid conflict. Instead of gently pointing out how someone hurt us, we often hold on to the pain and let it turn into anger or hate. When we hate, we become the ones sinning against God and hurt our own spiritual growth.

Rather than hold a grudge, lovingly try to reconcile with the person who hurt you. They may not be open to making up, but your conscience will be clear knowing you did your part to maintain peace.

Father God, I know it's wrong to hate someone in my heart. Give me the right words to say when someone hurts me, and help me let go of any anger if they aren't sorry for what they've done.

Day 93

Jesus Is "God with Us"

"She will give birth to a son, and they will call him Immanuel, which means 'God is with us.'"

Matthew 1:23 NLT

The name for Jesus, Immanuel, means "God is with us," which is so encouraging. Remembering and celebrating the fact that Jesus came to be here on earth with us and knows our struggles and fears as human beings firsthand is comforting. God is with us every moment. No, we weren't alive during Jesus' time as a human on earth, but we trust that He was here and experienced a human life like we are now. And today we have His Word and the Holy Spirit to help us live for Him until our time on earth is finished or He returns again, whichever comes first.

Jesus Immanuel, You understand me because You came to be a human and lived in this world too. Please help me trust, depend on, and relate to You more each day. Amen.

Day 94

Jesus' Mother, Mary

The angel said to her, "Mary, do not be afraid. You have found favor with God. See! You are to become a mother and have a Son. You are to give Him the name Jesus."
LUKE 1:30–31 NLV

When Mary was told she would be the mother of Jesus, she was scared and confused at first. But once her questions were answered, she said, "I am willing to be used of the Lord. Let it happen to me as you have said" (Luke 1:38 NLV). And when she shared the news with her cousin Elizabeth, she said: "Oh, how my soul praises the Lord. How my spirit rejoices in God my Savior! For he took notice of his lowly servant girl, and from now on all generations will call me blessed. For the Mighty One is holy, and he has done great things for me. He shows mercy from generation to generation to all who fear him" (Luke 1:46–50 NLT).

Jesus, when You ask me to do big things, help me to worship You, thank You, and trust You to equip me to do exactly what You call me to. Amen.

Day 95

Jesus' Earthly Father, Joseph

[Jesus'] mother, Mary, was engaged to be married to Joseph. But before the marriage took place, while she was still a virgin, she became pregnant through the power of the Holy Spirit. Joseph, to whom she was engaged, was a righteous man and did not want to disgrace her publicly, so he decided to break the engagement quietly. As he considered this, an angel of the Lord appeared to him in a dream. "Joseph, son of David," the angel said, "do not be afraid to take Mary as your wife. For the child within her was conceived by the Holy Spirit. And she will have a son, and you are to name him Jesus, for he will save his people from their sins.". . . When Joseph woke up, he did as the angel of the Lord commanded and took Mary as his wife.

MATTHEW 1:18–21, 24 NLT

Joseph was clearly a good man. He had to have been very upset to learn Mary was pregnant when he knew the child wasn't his. Even so, he didn't want to disgrace Mary publicly. But as he considered what to do, an angel appeared to him to explain everything and give him exact instructions. And Joseph willingly obeyed.

Jesus, I'm grateful for the example of Joseph. Help me to listen and obey You, even in unique situations that I don't fully understand. Amen.

Day 96

Because God First Loved Us

We, though, are going to love—love and be loved. First we were loved, now we love. He loved us first.

1 John 4:19 MSG

Your ability and desire to love is because you were first loved by God. He introduced you to the feeling. He made it come alive in your heart. God is the one who showered you with His goodness, helping you understand what compassion and care look like. And because love has bloomed in you, you're able to pass it along.

That's why you can muster kindness to siblings that drive you nuts. It's why you can forgive and ask for forgiveness from friends. Love is why you can't stay mad at your parents when they discipline. And it's why your heart is full of empathy and concern for those who are hurting. So keep choosing love, friend. You can access it anytime. The world needs God's love flowing through you toward others.

Lord, thank You for loving me first and giving me the perfect example of what it looks like. With Your divine help, I want to always choose to love others. Amen.

Day 97

King Jesus

For a child is born to us, a son is given to us. The government will rest on his shoulders. . . . His government and its peace will never end. He will rule with fairness and justice from the throne of his ancestor David for all eternity. The passionate commitment of the Lord *of Heaven's Armies will make this happen!*

Isaiah 9:6–7 NLT

Jesus is coming back! When He returns, He will establish a kingdom of perfect peace—no more wars or corruption (Zechariah 9:10). He'll rule with perfect fairness and justice. Everyone on earth will worship Him, and His kingdom will never be destroyed (Daniel 7:14). Sounds like heaven! Because it will be.

The world around us is decaying rapidly. Sin's ugly influence is everywhere. It's easy to lose hope that things will ever turn around or be fair or right. But they will be! God promises. We can keep our hope and confidence in Him. One day He *will* come back and restore all things.

Jesus, I can't wait for Your return! As the world falls apart, help me remain at peace, because one day You will make all things right.

Day 98

Keep Rejoicing

Beloved, do not be surprised at the fiery ordeal among you, which comes upon you for your testing, as though something strange were happening to you; but to the degree that you share the sufferings of Christ, keep on rejoicing, so that at the revelation of His glory you may also rejoice and be overjoyed.

1 PETER 4:12–13 NASB

When we live for Christ and put Him first, we don't fit in with the world. We seem like oddballs. That creates a lot of problems for us. People don't understand us. They may make fun of us or exclude us from their groups. That stinks, but God says we shouldn't be surprised when it happens. We're not really a part of this world. We're not supposed to fit in.

Look for others like you. They are there; they just may be in the background. And find joy in the journey—because God sees, and He will bless you.

Help me live for You, even when it's hard. Send me friends who want to live for You too.

Day 99

Known

Lord, you have examined me and know all about me. You know when I sit down and when I get up. You know my thoughts before I think them. You know where I go and where I lie down. You know everything I do. Lord, even before I say a word, you already know it.

Psalm 139:1–4 NCV

When you feel misunderstood or unknown, misheard or unseen, stop yourself. No matter how people make you feel, it's time to examine what is true.

The truth is that the Lord knows everything about you. He understands you. He knows you absolutely and completely. He knows when you get up and when you sit down. He knows when you sleep and when you wake. He knows what you're thinking, He knows what you'll say, and He knows what you've already said. He hears every single prayer you pray. He sees you, He hears you, He knows you. . .and He loves you.

Lord, it's amazing to realize that You know absolutely everything about me and choose to love me.

Day 100

Don't Hate

If someone says, "I love God," but hates a fellow believer, that person is a liar; for if we don't love people we can see, how can we love God, whom we cannot see?

1 John 4:20 NLT

If you're able to love God with all your heart but hate those around you—even if it feels justified—let it be a red flag. There may be those who you deeply disagree with. Maybe someone hurt you in significant ways. You may struggle to connect with offensive people, mean-spirited in what they do or say. And there may be differences too big to overcome. But the Lord doesn't see the justification in hating them.

Rather than take that strong stance, spend time with God. Ask Him to help you set appropriate and healthy boundaries to keep you emotionally safe. Commit to pray for your enemies, asking Him to let you see them through His eyes. Choosing to love and not curse keeps your heart from becoming hard and bitter. And it proves your love for God is authentic.

Lord, help me love others no matter what. Amen.

Day 101

Picking Favorites

If a man enters your church wearing an expensive suit, and a street person wearing rags comes in right after him, and you say to the man in the suit, "Sit here, sir; this is the best seat in the house!" and either ignore the street person or say, "Better sit here in the back row," haven't you segregated God's children and proved that you are judges who can't be trusted?

James 2:2–4 MSG

Think about how excited you'd be if your favorite actor or athlete came and sat next to you at church. You'd be thrilled, and if you weren't too starstruck, you'd probably want to help them connect and make sure they felt welcome. (And maybe snag a selfie with them.)

Would you greet a stranger who dressed or acted oddly with that same excitement and enthusiasm? Would you make sure they felt welcome and included? Christian kindness means stepping outside your comfort zone and making sure everyone—both rich and poor, cool and uncool, famous and unknown—feels welcome and loved.

Dear Jesus, I don't want to show partiality. I need to see and welcome everyone as if they were the most important person I've met.

Day 102

Let Jesus Lead You

The LORD is my shepherd, I lack nothing. He makes me lie down in green pastures, he leads me beside quiet waters, he refreshes my soul. He guides me along the right paths for his name's sake. Even though I walk through the darkest valley, I will fear no evil, for you are with me; your rod and your staff, they comfort me. You prepare a table before me in the presence of my enemies. You anoint my head with oil; my cup overflows. Surely your goodness and love will follow me all the days of my life, and I will dwell in the house of the LORD forever.

PSALM 23 NIV

The Bible tells us how the Lord is our shepherd guiding and protecting us through all of life's ups and downs. He gives us all the peace and security, goodness and love that we need.

Jesus, I'd be so lost without You!
Thank You for being my good shepherd.

Day 103

Relational God

"The virgin will conceive and give birth to a son, and they will call him Immanuel" (which means "God with us").

MATTHEW 1:23 NIV

God's greatest desire has always been to be with us. He walked with Adam and Eve in the garden of Eden at the beginning of creation (Genesis 2:8). When sin wrecked that closeness, He drew near to humanity in other ways: leading the Israelites by a pillar of cloud and fire (Exodus 13:21–22), dwelling physically in the tabernacle and temple (Exodus 40:34–38; 1 Kings 8:10–11), becoming a man who walked and lived among us, and giving us the Holy Spirit who lives inside us (John 14:16–17). One day He will create a new heaven and earth where He can live with us forever (Revelation 21:3). Do you see how much God *longs* for relationship with you? He'll remove all barriers, fight any battles, and take any risks in order to be with you. You can count on it!

God, it's humbling to know You so badly want a relationship with *me*. Help me draw close to You too.

Day 104

Olympic Training

In this you greatly rejoice, even though now for a little while, if necessary, you have been distressed by various trials, so that the proof of your faith, being more precious than gold which perishes though tested by fire, may be found to result in praise, glory, and honor at the revelation of Jesus Christ.

1 Peter 1:6–7 NASB

Have you ever watched the Olympics? Those athletes didn't just wake up one morning and decide, "I think I'll be an Olympic champion." Anyone who's been chosen to represent their country in that way has put in hours of practice. They've gotten up early and worked late. They've sweated, endured bruises and sore muscles, and given up lots of social opportunities. The glory—the medal—comes only after all the hardship.

Right now, you're in training for God's Olympic event. One day, if you keep going, you'll share in His glory, and He'll give you a crown. Don't give up.

> I know You have great plans for my life, Lord. When I go through hard things, remind me that I'm in training for something better.

Day 105

Kindness in All Things

For I can do everything through Christ, who gives me strength.
PHILIPPIANS 4:13 NLT

The apostle Paul, who wrote this verse in his letter to the Philippian church, experienced all kinds of circumstances during his ministry. He went through times with plenty and times with nothing. He experienced persecution and acceptance. He knew that whatever he faced, he could do it with the strength of Christ.

Some days kindness will come easily. Other days, you won't feel like being kind at all. You'll be tired, sick, or in a bad mood and tempted to take out your frustrations on the people around you. In those moments, rely on the strength of Christ to help you love others.

Dear God, give me Your strength on difficult days. Even when I'm having a hard time, make me obedient to Your call for kindness.

Day 106

Give Your Worries and Cares to Jesus

Give all your cares to the Lord and He will give you strength.
He will never let those who are right with Him be shaken.
PSALM 55:22 NLV

Jesus is Lord over all of your worries and fears. He promises that those who are right with Him will never be shaken. (You are right with Him when you have chosen Jesus as your Savior.) What are you worried about today? What feels shaky in your life? What are you not feeling sure about? Let the Lord take those things away from you and give you His strength, peace, and power instead. We can trust Him to take care of it all.

Jesus, I don't know why I hold on to worries so often, when You've told me You want to take them away from me and give me strength instead. Please help me give my anxiety to You! I want to trust You more and have more of Your perfect peace and power. Amen.

Day 107

The Word

In the beginning was the one who is called the Word. The Word was with God and was truly God. . . . The Word became a human being and lived here with us. We saw his true glory, the glory of the only Son of the Father. From him the complete gifts of undeserved grace and truth have come down to us.

John 1:1, 14 CEV

Christian lingo says you need to "have a relationship with Jesus." But how do you have a relationship with someone you can't see?! And how do you know if it's God speaking to you or if it's the ham and cheese you ate for dinner messing with you?! Relax, friend. You can have a relationship with Jesus—even though you can't see Him—through His Word, the Bible. Jesus *is* the Word. The Word *is* Jesus. So know the Word. . .and you know Jesus. Spending time reading the Word is spending time with Jesus. The more you know Him, the more confident you'll be in your relationship with Him.

Jesus, I want to know You better. Bless the time I spend in Your Word, showing me who You are.

Day 108

Everything I Need

We are afflicted in every way, but not crushed; perplexed, but not despairing; persecuted, but not abandoned; struck down, but not destroyed.

2 Corinthians 4:8–9 NASB

Wouldn't it be great if being a Christian were easy? If choosing right and living for God were popular, if it brought immediate pleasure, then everyone would do it. But most things that have value aren't easy. Most things that are worthwhile in the end take some work to get there.

The good news is, God never leaves us alone in the journey. We may go through hard times, but He's right beside us, giving us strength to endure. We may face tough decisions, but He's right there coaching us, directing us, and showing us the way. Stay close to Him. Hold tight to His love. He will never leave you, and He will give you everything you need to succeed.

Thank You for giving me the things I need to live out Your purpose for me.

Day 109

Peace Be with You All

The God who gives peace be with you all. Amen.
ROMANS 15:33 NCV

When you pray, it can be easy to focus on your own concerns. After all, you know what you're facing. You know how you feel. You know what you want to talk with God about.

Yet it's important to pray for other people too. Pray for those you love. Pray for your family members and friends. Pray for people you don't know very well. Pray for people you don't know at all.

When you pray for others, don't limit yourself to only asking certain requests they may have asked you. Pray bigger prayers. Pray that God would fill their lives with His peace. Pray that God would be with them and guide them. Pray the Lord would work in their lives in amazing ways.

As you pray these bold prayers, know you're trusting in the Lord to do good not only in your own life but also in the lives of others.

Father, I praise You for being the God who gives peace. Help me see who I need to pray for today.

Day 110

Unselfish Love

He has given us this command: Those who love God must also love their fellow believers.

1 John 4:21 NLT

If God commands you to love unselfishly, then rest assured He will give you the ability to do so. As mere humans, we're incapable of it. Alone, it's impossible. But when you ask the Lord to fill your heart with generosity toward others, He will. When you ask for kindness to be your default button, it will happen. And when faced with a difficult situation and you ask God to help you be selfless as you navigate it, He will bless you.

So often we think it's all up to us. We put pressure on ourselves to be the perfect Christian girl who always responds with grace and love. Talk about pressure! But when we realize grace and love come from God above, it brings freedom from our unrealistic expectations. While we still must choose love, He is the one who give us the ability.

Lord, help me love others unselfishly by filling me with the desire and divine power to do so. Amen.

Day 111

Let Jesus Make His Home in Your Heart

Christ will make his home in your hearts as you trust in him. Your roots will grow down into God's love and keep you strong. And may you have the power to understand, as all God's people should, how wide, how long, how high, and how deep his love is. May you experience the love of Christ, though it is too great to understand fully. Then you will be made complete with all the fullness of life and power that comes from God.

Ephesians 3:17–19 NLT

The world will tell you all kinds of ways to be a strong young woman, but real, eternal strength comes from Jesus. As you trust in Him, He makes His home in your heart, and you grow stronger every day that you continue to choose Him. Like a tree with good roots, you won't be toppled and broken during the storms of life.

Jesus, help me focus on how incredible and endless Your love for me is! And help me keep on growing stronger every day with You in my heart. Amen.

Day 112

Avoid Sinful Things

I will set no sinful thing in front of my eyes. I hate the work of those who are not faithful. It will not get hold of me. A sinful heart will be far from me. I will have nothing to do with sin.

Psalm 101:3–4 NLV

The writer of this psalm makes a big promise in this passage. It was easier in his time to make that promise because there were no movies, television shows, smartphones, and social media back then. So we have to be extra careful with what we pay attention to these days because the world is full of sinful things that we can see so easily—and our enemy, the devil, wants to push every sinful thing on us so that we will walk away from following Jesus.

Jesus, I want to make this promise too—I don't want to look at or watch anything that is sinful. I want to keep my mind and heart clean and far away from sin. I need a lot of help with this. Please help me. Amen.

Day 113

Bread of Life

Jesus replied, "I am the bread of life. Whoever comes to me will never be hungry again. Whoever believes in me will never be thirsty."

John 6:35 NLT

Jesus fed five thousand people with five loaves of bread. Hungry again, that same crowd went searching for Jesus the next day. Jesus scolded them for working so hard to find Him just for another free meal. He's good for more than a physical handout. When we seek Him with spiritual hunger, He will always satisfy us. (Read the whole story in John 6.)

Meeting physical needs is only a temporary fix. Our real and lasting problem is our spiritual state: Who will we depend on to find forgiveness, peace, and eternal life? Only Jesus can provide those things with an unending supply. Don't get me wrong, God loves to give gifts to His children and meet our physical wants and needs (Matthew 7:11)! But most importantly, we should seek Him with our spiritual needs. He is the Bread of Life, who can supply *all* our needs—physical, emotional, and spiritual!

Jesus, I come to You today not just seeking physical things but desiring You to feed my soul too.

Day 114

Persevere

Blessed is a man who perseveres under trial; for once he has been approved, he will receive the crown of life which the Lord has promised to those who love Him.

James 1:12 NASB

Everybody goes through hard stuff. Those are called trials, and they're not any fun. When faced with difficult times, many people will give up. They'll decide it's not worth the trouble and just quit on their Christian walk.

But good things come to those who wait. The Bible talks a lot about waiting. Another word for *wait* might be *persevere*. Hold tight. Don't give up.

Those who hang in there, who make the hard choices, who keep loving God and serving Him even when no one else does. . .those people are blessed. God sees, and He takes note. Hold on! One day, you'll see. God will make sure it's worth it for you in the end.

Help me persevere today, Lord. It's hard, but I know You're with me, giving me strength.

Day 115

Searching

God, you are my God. I search for you. I thirst for you like someone in a dry, empty land where there is no water. I have seen you in the Temple and have seen your strength and glory. Because your love is better than life, I will praise you. I will praise you as long as I live.

Psalm 63:1–4 NCV

Each day, it may feel like you need to search for God. Circumstances may seem less than ideal, and you have to really look to find God in the moment. When you find Him, you'll notice He hasn't changed. He's still the God who has infinite strength and glory. He's still the God who loves you with a love that's even better than life.

This God is right there waiting for you. Praise Him for all the amazing and wonderful things you appreciate about Him. Lift up your hands and praise Him because He is a God who can be found.

God, You are my God. I am so glad that when I search for You, I can find You.

Day 116

But Love Covers

Hatred stirs up quarrels, but love makes up for all offenses.
PROVERBS 10:12 NLT

God's desire is for us to forgive others rather than hold on to our hurt or anger. Even more, we're called to overlook their faults because we love them. It's deciding our relationship means more than holding a grudge. It's choosing to cut someone a break for being imperfect. It's letting them off the hook for making mistakes. It's allowing grace to flow freely, covering the wrongdoing with love instead. And it takes God's help.

Today, tell God about your struggles with this. Talk to Him about the friends, family, teachers, coaches, and coworkers who make forgiving hard to do. Ask for a greater measure of compassion to offset the anger that often invades your heart and mind. And ask for the strength to choose love over unforgiveness so you can live in peace with others.

Lord, it's hard to overlook the hurt and frustration that others cause. It's hard to let love speak louder. So please give me the desire and ability to follow Your command. Amen.

Day 117

Beautiful Mercy

There will be no mercy for those who have not shown mercy to others. But if you have been merciful, God will be merciful when he judges you.

James 2:13 NLT

If you struggle to show compassion, take a moment and meditate on the incredible mercy you've been shown by God. Instead of leaving you to wallow in your sins, God extended compassion and mercy. He entered the messiness of the world by sending Jesus to live perfectly, die horrifically, and conquer death with the resurrection. Because of this, nothing you've done will be held against you if you put your trust in Christ. You're a completely forgiven child of God!

This is great mercy, and a person who's been *shown* great mercy *shows* great mercy to others.

Heavenly Father, help me show compassion and mercy to all who need it.

Day 118

The Beatitudes

"Blessed are the poor in spirit, for theirs is the kingdom of heaven. Blessed are those who mourn, for they will be comforted. Blessed are the meek, for they will inherit the earth. Blessed are those who hunger and thirst for righteousness, for they will be filled. Blessed are the merciful, for they will be shown mercy. Blessed are the pure in heart, for they will see God. Blessed are the peacemakers, for they will be called children of God. Blessed are those who are persecuted because of righteousness, for theirs is the kingdom of heaven. Blessed are you when people insult you, persecute you and falsely say all kinds of evil against you because of me. Rejoice and be glad, because great is your reward in heaven."

MATTHEW 5:3–12 NIV

Jesus' words in this well-known passage of the Bible called the Beatitudes sound pretty much opposite from what the world tells us will make us happy. Despite the popular messages of our day, wealth, fame, and power are not real sources of blessing. Instead, we are truly blessed and happy when we are humble and do the will of God, loving Him above all and caring for others.

Jesus, please provide me with the blessings You say are best of all. Amen.

Day 119

Light of the World

Jesus spoke to the people once more and said, "I am the light of the world. If you follow me, you won't have to walk in darkness, because you will have the light that leads to life."

John 8:12 NLT

Without Jesus, we walk in spiritual darkness and death. But Jesus shines His light on our hearts so we can understand and know who God is and the path He wants us to follow (2 Corinthians 4:6). How do you need Jesus to shed light in your life? Do spiritual questions niggle and require answers? Are you struggling with a decision or situation and need some guidance? Are there secrets or sin you're keeping in the dark that should be brought into the light of confession and forgiveness?

Walking in the light brings freedom and blessing (Psalm 27:1; 84:11; 89:15). *But*, you ask, *how do I know what God wants me to do?* God's peace will guard you (Philippians 4:7). When God's peace fills you, you know you are walking in the light.

Jesus, I need Your light today. Show me the steps to take, and surround me with Your peace.

Day 120

Brokenhearted

When the righteous cry for help, the LORD hears and delivers them out of all their troubles. The LORD is near to the brokenhearted and saves the crushed in spirit.

PSALM 34:17–18 ESV

Has your heart been broken? It may be over a boy or a bruised friendship or your parents' divorce. Maybe you didn't get the part you wanted in the school play, or perhaps you're facing a difficult health diagnosis. No matter the reason, God is there. He never belittles your feelings. Instead, He holds you in His arms. He sends His Holy Spirit to comfort you.

Whatever you're facing today, call out to your Father. Tell Him what's on your mind. He loves you more than you can imagine, and He won't leave you to cry alone. He's right there, and He will bring you through this to a better place.

Father, my heart is broken right now. You know the reasons. Thank You for listening, for understanding, and for holding me close as I cry. I trust You to bring me through this.

Day 121

Sinking Deep

While Jonah was inside the fish, he prayed to the Lord his God and said, "When I was in danger, I called to the Lord, and he answered me. I was about to die, so I cried to you, and you heard my voice. You threw me into the sea, down, down into the deep sea."

Jonah 2:1–3 NCV

God had a specific mission for Jonah to accomplish, yet Jonah ran away to avoid obeying God. His attempt to flee only ended in disaster: he was thrown off a ship in a storm and sank before being swallowed by a big fish. Even with all that adventure, Jonah didn't die. Instead, he prayed while he was sinking and near death, and he prayed while spending three days inside the fish.

While you may never end up in a fish, you'll disobey or even try to run from God at some point. Once you realize you should follow and obey the Lord, pray! Pray when it feels like you're sinking deep. Pray when you need a second chance. Pray when it feels like you're drowning.

Father, some days it feels like I'm sinking in life. Please help me!

Day 122

With All You Have

Jesus said, "The first in importance is, 'Listen, Israel: The Lord your God is one; so love the Lord God with all your passion and prayer and intelligence and energy.'"

Mark 12:29–30 msg

As believers, we should choose to love God with all we have. It's an intentional decision to focus our life on loving and honoring Him in meaningful ways. It isn't easy to do, but Jesus says it is important. How are you doing with that?

How do you love God with your passion? Do you let His Word burn in your heart and let it flow into your day from there? Are you loving the Lord through prayer, talking with Him on the regular about anything and everything? Do you meditate on scripture, finding ways to let its wisdom help you choose wisely? And do you give your relationship with God concentrated time, energy, and connection?

Friend, when you choose to love God with all you have, it will bless you and glorify Him. And it will help you live and love those around you with passion and purpose too.

Lord, help me love You with all I am. . .every day. Amen.

Day 123

Hating Evil

Love must be free of hypocrisy.
Detest what is evil; cling to what is good.
ROMANS 12:9 NASB

We're sometimes taught that it's wrong to hate, but it's actually *good* to hate things God hates. Murder, oppression, injustice, and sin all deserve our hatred and disgust. These things offend and grieve God. Therefore, they should offend and grieve us as well.

If we claim to love people but ignore suffering and injustice, our love looks hypocritical to the world. By hating what's evil, we express love to those who've been wronged. Righteous anger drives us to speak up and act on behalf of those victimized and marginalized. It drives us to shine our light in the darkest places.

Lord God, teach me to recognize and hate evil. Help me cling to what's good and look for ways to destroy what's wicked in Your eyes.

Day 124

Worship Jesus

Make a joyful noise to the LORD, all the earth! Serve the LORD with gladness! Come into his presence with singing! Know that the LORD, he is God! It is he who made us, and we are his; we are his people, and the sheep of his pasture. Enter his gates with thanksgiving, and his courts with praise! Give thanks to him; bless his name! For the LORD is good; his steadfast love endures forever, and his faithfulness to all generations.

PSALM 100 ESV

With psalms like this and your favorite hymns, worship Jesus! Anytime, anywhere! Even when you need to be quiet, you can focus on praising Jesus in your mind, and immediately you'll be filled with goodness and joy.

Jesus, I am Yours! I want to praise You everywhere I go in everything I do! You are so good and so amazing! Your love is endless, and I'm so grateful. Amen.

Day 125

The Gate

"I am the gate for the sheep. . . . Those who come in through me will be saved. They will come and go freely and will find good pastures. The thief's purpose is to steal and kill and destroy. My purpose is to give them a rich and satisfying life."

John 10:7, 9–10 NLT

Jesus gave an analogy and compared Himself to the gate of a sheep pen. There's only one way in and out of that pen—the gate. Anyone who tries to climb into the pen another way only intends to harm the sheep (John 10:1).

Many people and religions offer ways to God—but they are lies intended to harm you, the sheep. Satan wants to rob you of the life Jesus offers. "Come out from the pen," he whispers. "This pen is too restricting. There's a better pen over there with more freedom! Ditch this place." But you can be confident the salvation Jesus offers is the only freedom and satisfaction you'll find.

Jesus, sometimes what the world tells me sounds a whole lot better than Your way. Help me recognize the lies so I can stay under Your life-giving care.

Day 126

Bad Day

Answer me quickly, O Lord! My spirit fails! Hide not your face from me, lest I be like those who go down to the pit. Let me hear in the morning of your steadfast love, for in you I trust. Make me know the way I should go, for to you I lift up my soul.

Psalm 143:7–8 ESV

Have you ever had a really bad day—so bad that you couldn't sleep that night? Those kinds of days are, unfortunately, part of life. Crying ourselves to sleep is an awful way to end the day. Next time you have one of those days or weeks or months, talk to God.

Remind God that you love Him no matter what and that you'll praise Him even in the hard times. Ask Him to get you through this season quickly and to let tomorrow be a better day. He hears, and He cares more than you can ever imagine.

I need You, Father. Help me through this hard time. Please make tomorrow a better day. I love You with all my heart.

Day 127

Who Gets the Glory?

Not to us, Lord, not to us but to your name be the glory, because of your love and faithfulness.

Psalm 115:1 NIV

Someone gets glory for things that are accomplished. In your life, who usually gets the glory? Do you take credit when the spotlight shines on you? Do you give credit to someone else? Or do you choose to give all the glory to God?

When you see the Lord working and acting in your life and in the world, don't be afraid to give God the glory. Give Him praise. Give Him credit. Because of His love and faithfulness, He works in amazing ways. Whether it's through the things you say or the prayers you pray, shine the spotlight on the Lord. Give Him glory and thanks and praise for working in His amazing ways.

Father, I give You all the glory! You have worked in a wonderful way because of Your love and faithfulness. I praise You!

Day 128

Love Others the Same

"The second is equally important: 'Love your neighbor as yourself.' No other commandment is greater than these."
Mark 12:31 NLT

What are some of the ways you are kind to yourself? Chances are you do things that make you feel good, like eat well, exercise, and get plenty of sleep. Maybe you buy yourself items that delight your heart. Do you set aside downtime if necessary or pack your days if you're more of an extrovert? Do you make sure your basic needs are met each day? Friend, how do you love yourself?

The Lord says the time and attention we take to be good to ourselves should also be taken to be good toward others. It's His desire for you to love those around you like you love yourself. It's not necessarily in the exact same ways but in your heart and motive. It's a call to not put yourself above others. It's choosing to love them with the same passion and purpose. And even more, it's God's command.

Lord, help me choose to love others like I love myself. Let my heart always be for them. Amen.

Day 129

What Are Your Motives?

Do nothing from selfish ambition or conceit, but in humility count others more significant than yourselves.

PHILIPPIANS 2:3 ESV

"Aim higher! Push harder! Accomplish more!" This is a common message in today's world. We're told to get to the top, no matter the cost.

God's given you unique talents and goals. It's always a good idea, however, to do a "heart check" and ask yourself *why* you want to achieve something. Do you want to be a singer because you desire fame, money, and glory? Or did God give you an amazing voice and you love using your gift and sharing it with others?

Selfish motives will make you see other people as something to be used in order to achieve your own goals. Godly motives help you see the value of every human being, whether or not they play a role in your success.

Father God, I thank You for giving me my talents. Reveal to me any selfish motives, and help me value the gifts of those around me more than my own.

Day 130

Jesus' Cousin John

In those days John the Baptist came preaching in the desert in the country of Judea. He said, "Be sorry for your sins and turn from them! The holy nation of heaven is near." The early preacher Isaiah spoke of this man. He said, "Listen! His voice calls out in the desert! 'Make the way ready for the Lord. Make the road straight for Him!'"

MATTHEW 3:1–3 NLV

Jesus' cousin was John the Baptist. He was an interesting guy! His "clothes were made of camel's hair, and he had a leather belt around his waist. His food was locusts and wild honey" (Matthew 3:4 NIV). He preached to people about the kingdom of heaven and prepared the way for Jesus' ministry. He baptized people but pointed to Jesus, saying, "I baptize with water those who are sorry for their sins and turn from them. The One Who comes after me will baptize you with the Holy Spirit and with fire. He is greater than I. I am not good enough to take off His shoes" (Matthew 3:11 NLV).

Jesus, thank You for teaching me more about You through John the Baptist's ministry.

Day 131

The Good Shepherd

"I am the good shepherd. The good shepherd sacrifices his life for the sheep."
John 10:11 NLT

Jesus willingly died for you (John 10:18). The suffering of the cross was more bearable to Him than the suffering of being separated from you forever because of your sin. That's a deep love!

Because of that love, Jesus fiercely fights for you. When Satan comes sneaking around as a wolf in sheep's clothing, Jesus exposes the lies and frees you from harm. If Satan has led you astray, Jesus will search until He finds you (Matthew 18:12–13). Jesus is the *good* shepherd. He only wants the best for you. Will you come under His gentle care and let Him lead you today?

Jesus, thank You for caring for me so deeply. Thank You for always fighting for me, protecting me, and never leaving me. Help me see Your goodness and love when I want to struggle against You. Help me place my confidence and security in You instead of trying to do things my way.

Day 132

The Thief

"The thief comes only to steal and kill and destroy. I came that they may have life and have it abundantly."

John 10:10 ESV

The thief Jesus talks about here is Satan. He's a tricky fellow. He has ways of making you think the only way you'll be happy is to go against God's ways. But he's a liar. He wants to steal your joy, your peace, and your innocence. He wants to lead you down a hole so deep, you'll wonder if you'll ever find your way out.

Christ is truth. He will never lie to you, and He always keeps His promises. Here, He tells us that He is the way to an abundant life full of love, laughter, joy, and peace. Next time you're tempted to do something you know God doesn't want you to do, remember who loves you so much He gave His life for you. Follow Him.

Thank You for this reminder that Satan is a liar and that he wants to destroy my life. I want to follow You.

Day 133

Life Without Fear

Even if I walk through a very dark valley,
I will not be afraid, because you are with me.
Your rod and your shepherd's staff comfort me.
PSALM 23:4 NCV

The Lord is your shepherd. He willingly and lovingly guides you through all the good and all the bad parts of life. The comforting thing is that He'll never leave you. Even when it seems like your life's path is rocky or unstable, He's there. He's with you. You don't have to be afraid.

When fear comes rushing in, threatening to take over your thoughts, tell your Father. Talk with Him about what seems to threaten your peace of mind. You can honestly tell Him how you feel, knowing He's there to gently comfort you.

Lord, knowing You are my shepherd is a huge relief.
I don't need to try to figure things out on my own.
No matter how alone I feel, You are with me.
I choose not to live in fear, because You are God.

Day 134

No Fear of God

We need have no fear of someone who loves us perfectly; his perfect love for us eliminates all dread of what he might do to us. If we are afraid, it is for fear of what he might do to us and shows that we are not fully convinced that he really loves us.

1 John 4:18 TLB

At every turn, God chooses love. While He has every right and reason to punish, the Lord loves us perfectly. That doesn't mean we'll be saved from the natural consequences of our sins. He won't make life easy and pain-free. And we will face challenging seasons with friends and family. But in His great love, He will be there to help us walk through the difficulties ahead.

When you mess up, go right to God. There's no reason to be afraid of His wrath because we can be confident in His love. We can be convinced we're fully accepted. And we can choose to embrace this truth every day.

Lord, thank You for being a safe place where I'm loved perfectly! Amen.

Day 135

Curb the Complaining

Do everything without complaining and arguing.
PHILIPPIANS 2:14 NLT

Think about the last time you had to do something you really, really didn't want to do. Did you do it joyfully? Or did you complain and grumble the whole time?

Nothing brings down a situation faster than complaining and bickering. In fact, the smallest drop of whining or arguing can poison an entire experience. It throws our attitude into a tailspin of dissatisfaction. The opposite of complaining is gratitude, and a dash of thankfulness can defuse even the toughest situation.

If you're not careful, complaining can become your default attitude. Try to see every situation as an opportunity to glorify God. By expressing thanks in all things, even if it's not what you want, you'll rip a complaining spirit out by its roots.

Lord, please help me do things with joy and gratitude. I don't want to be a complainer!

Day 136

Jesus' First Disciples

As Jesus was walking beside the Sea of Galilee, he saw two brothers, Simon called Peter and his brother Andrew. They were casting a net into the lake, for they were fishermen. "Come, follow me," Jesus said, "and I will send you out to fish for people." At once they left their nets and followed him. Going on from there, he saw two other brothers, James son of Zebedee and his brother John. They were in a boat with their father Zebedee, preparing their nets. Jesus called them, and immediately they left the boat and their father and followed him.

MATTHEW 4:18–22 NIV

Jesus chose humble, regular people to call to be His first disciples. They were just fishermen, not royalty, government officials, or wealthy people. Jesus called them to a new type of fishing job—fishing for people who would also want to join in following Jesus. Notice how "at once" and "immediately" these men came to Jesus. We should be inspired to also obey Jesus so quickly when He calls.

Jesus, thank You for the first disciples' example of obedience to You. Thank You for calling humble people to You to be saved. Amen.

Day 137

Hanging Out

"You keep him in perfect peace whose mind is stayed on you, because he trusts in you."

Isaiah 26:3 ESV

Have you ever wanted something so much that you couldn't think of anything else? That's what the author of this verse is talking about. When we love God so much that He's all we think about, He gives us peace. That doesn't mean we don't do our homework or our chores because we're thinking about God. It means that while we're doing those things, we include Him. We talk to Him inside our minds. We ask Him to help us find that lost backpack. We consult Him about how to handle a hard situation or a rude person.

God wants to hang out with us all the time. When you choose to think about Him, talk about Him, and hang out with Him in your heart, He gives you peace.

> Father, I want You more than anything. Walk with me every minute of every day. Remind me of Your presence. I want to hang out with You.

Day 138

The Resurrection and Life

Jesus told her, "I am the resurrection and the life. Anyone who believes in me will live, even after dying."
John 11:25 NLT

Mary and Martha, close friends of Jesus, sent word to Him that their brother was deathly ill. Jesus delayed coming to see them, and Lazarus died. When Jesus finally arrived, He found the sisters weeping in grief. This intensely moved and distressed Him (John 11:33). The original Greek word carries the meaning of anger: Jesus was deeply indignant or angry. At what? The sisters? No, death itself. He fumed about the tragic results of Adam's sin (Romans 5:12). He found Himself surrounded by the pain and consequences of Satan's evil—and He got *ticked*. "You don't get to win, Satan! I won't let you take them from Me," Jesus seemed to say. He brought Lazarus back to life, and He made a way for *all* of us to receive eternal life.

He defeated death forever (1 Corinthians 15:54–55). That's the God we serve!

God, thank You for the hope of eternal life. Thank You for grieving with us and comforting us when we face the physical death of loved ones.

Day 139

The End of the Story

"I have said these things to you, that in me you may have peace. In the world you will have tribulation. But take heart; I have overcome the world."

John 16:33 ESV

Do you ever read a few chapters of a book then flip to the end to see how it turns out? Most novels are filled with difficult times for the main character. If things were too easy, the story would be dull. But it usually works out well in the end.

As Christians, we get to know the end of the story. Christ wins. *We* win! We'll face hard times in this journey called life, but we can face those times with a knowing smile, with confidence that it'll all work out in the end. In the meantime, as we stay close to God, He promises to give us everything we need for a full, abundant life.

Thank You for reminding me of how Your story ends. I want to stay close to You during my journey here, in good times and bad. I trust You completely.

Day 140

No Stumbling

To him who is able to keep you from stumbling and to present you before his glorious presence without fault and with great joy—to the only God our Savior be glory, majesty, power and authority, through Jesus Christ our Lord, before all ages, now and forevermore! Amen.

JUDE 24–25 NIV

Sometimes it feels like you're stumbling, bumbling, and mumbling through life. As much as you try to do what's right, you stumble into sin. When it comes time to make a decision, you don't know what you should do, so you bumble around with uncertainty. And some days you mumble the wrong thing or have no idea what to say.

Good news! You don't have to sweat all your missteps. God loves you, and He's able to keep you from stumbling. At the end of your life, because of your faith in Jesus Christ, you'll be in His glorious presence without fault and with great joy. When you pray, remind yourself of these truths, and thank God for each one.

> Lord, it's absolutely amazing to know You work in my heart and my life. Thank You for keeping me from stumbling! I praise You!

Day 141

Strength

Then Samson prayed to the Lord, "Lord God, remember me. God, please give me strength one more time so I can pay these Philistines back for putting out my two eyes!"

Judges 16:28 NCV

Samson lived a life doing the Lord's purpose until he was distracted and tempted by Delilah. After he chose to follow his own way instead of the Lord's, he suffered greatly. In what would be his final work on this earth, Samson prayed for the Lord's strength so he could punish the Philistines. Samson would sacrifice his own life in this act, and he knew it was a suicide mission. Yet he knew the one who could provide enough strength to accomplish the task. He knew the one who could make the impossible possible.

Hopefully you won't be led astray like Samson. Hopefully you'll choose to live a life of devotion and obedience. But regardless of your life choices and obedience, don't forget you can always pray to the Lord to give you strength. You can always call on Him when you need Him the most.

Lord God, please give me strength to do Your good work!

Day 142

Pray for Your Enemies

"You have heard that it was said, 'You shall love your neighbor and hate your enemy.' But I say to you, love your enemies and pray for those who persecute you."
MATTHEW 5:43–44 NASB

During His ministry on earth, Jesus took time to correct false teachings that had emerged over the years. In this instance, spiritual leaders had been telling God's people that they had to love their neighbor but that hating their enemy was okay. Jesus corrects this error and raises the bar by telling them something baffling: love your neighbor, but love your enemy also!

Think about someone you'd consider an enemy. If *enemy* is too strong a word, think of a rival or bully. Can you pray sincerely that God blesses and prospers them? When we pray for those who don't treat us nicely, we give them a grace they don't know they're getting.

By blessing your enemy, you surrender to God a burden that will only weigh you down.

Lord, I ask that You bless those who treat me badly. I pray that they will come to know Your loving grace.

Day 143

New Creation

If anyone is in Christ, he is a new creation.
2 CORINTHIANS 5:17 ESV

When you get weighed down with all the things of this world and all the stress they can cause, you might feel like you need a new start and a new mindset. Does that sound good? When we choose Jesus as Savior, we become new creations, and He then blesses us with endless newness by His grace—for "if we confess our sins, he is faithful and just to forgive us our sins and to cleanse us from all unrighteousness" (1 John 1:9 ESV) and His mercies are new every morning (Lamentations 3:22–23).

Jesus, please help me to remember that I do not belong to this world. I belong to You! I am a new creation because I've chosen You to be my Savior. I want to live with joy and confidence in the facts that You cleanse me from sins when I confess them to You and that You give me new mercy every day. Amen.

Day 144

Plans

"For I know the plans that I have for you," declares the LORD, *"plans for prosperity and not for disaster, to give you a future and a hope."*

JEREMIAH 29:11 NASB

Do you ever look at God and say, "What were You thinking?" It's okay if you do. God already knows your thoughts, and He wants you to be honest with Him. The truth is, He was thinking of *you.* He was thinking of only the very best for you. Kind of like when your mom makes you eat food that you hate but that's good for you. She's not thinking about your preferences. She's thinking about your long-term health.

Your mom could give you your favorite junk food every day, anytime you wanted it, and you'd like it. But soon you'd start to feel bad, and your health would decline. She knows that, and she has your future in mind when she gives you healthy things. In the same way, God's thoughts are always for you, for a good and strong and abundant future. Trust Him.

Thank You for Your good plans for me. I trust You.

Day 145

The Way

Jesus told him, "I am the way, the truth, and the life. No one can come to the Father except through me."
John 14:6 NLT

Jesus stressed again that He's the only way to eternal life with the Father. Why did He keep repeating that? We get it already! But Jesus knew we'd need to hear it again and again—just like your mom often tells you to do something more than once, because she knows you're not really listening! In our human stubbornness, we don't want to accept there's only *one* way. We like to think we know better and can choose our own way. But Jesus reminds us again: "Nope, there's no other way but Me." You can fight it, deny it, and try to dance around it, but there's the plain, simple truth that will never change. Only His path is the right path. His truth is the correct truth. And His life is the real deal that satisfies. Have you accepted that?

Jesus, I surrender to You my desire to go my own way. Show me Your way and the life You offer.

Day 146

Practice Loving Others

Dear friends, let us practice loving each other, for love comes from God and those who are loving and kind show that they are the children of God, and that they are getting to know him better.

1 John 4:7 TLB

The closer you become to God, the better you love those around you. You will have more compassion for the hurting. You'll have more patience for the kids you babysit. You will care about others' feelings and act accordingly. You will model respect in the classroom and on the court. You won't be perfect, but you will be purposeful to love others well.

When you get the chance, practice loving one another. It may be messy at times. You may fail miserably. There may even be those who require every bit of your strength to show care and concern. But as you choose love, it will come easier. And it will reveal God's work in your life and in your heart.

Lord, let my relationship with You be evident in how I treat those around me. And help me always practice loving others in word and deed. Amen.

Day 147

Simple Gifts

"He causes his sun to rise on the evil and the good, and sends rain on the righteous and the unrighteous."
MATTHEW 5:45 NIV

God blesses both the saved and unsaved with common graces. Hope of a new day, seeing the glory of the sun setting behind the mountains, and watching waves crash onto the beach are all simple gifts everyone gets to enjoy.

As a child of God, you have the opportunity to show common grace to those around you. You can extend a smile, give a welcoming hello, share a meal, and offer a listening ear. Through these simple acts, many may come to know Jesus as King. Imagine the joy in knowing they'll receive eternal graces in addition to the temporary ones given in this life.

Father God, teach me to extend common grace to everyone around me, especially those who don't know You.

Day 148

Jesus Is the Bread of Life

Jesus said to the people, "For sure, I tell you, it was not Moses who gave you bread from heaven. My Father gives you the true Bread from heaven. The Bread of God is He Who comes down from heaven and gives life to the world." They said to Him, "Sir, give us this Bread all the time." Jesus said to them, "I am the Bread of Life. He who comes to Me will never be hungry. He who puts his trust in Me will never be thirsty."

John 6:32–35 NLV

Do you ever stop to think about how people lived without electricity, indoor plumbing, air-conditioning, or Wi-Fi? How on earth did they do it? It's hard to imagine life without our modern conveniences! But our most basic daily needs for life are food and water, right? So when Jesus calls Himself the "Bread of Life," did He mean that He expects us to believe in Him and then never eat food or drink water again? No. But Jesus does want us to trust in Him as the one who provides for all our needs. *He* is actually our most basic need because He gives us all life and eternal life!

Jesus, thank You for being everything I need. Amen.

Day 149

Peace

"Peace I leave you, My peace I give you; not as the world gives, do I give to you. Do not let your hearts be troubled, nor fearful."

JOHN 14:27 NASB

Many dictionaries define peace as the absence of war or trouble. But Christ told us that in this world we'd have trouble, so that definition doesn't fit. Peace, as the Bible describes it, isn't the absence of hardship. It's the presence of God.

According to this definition, we can have peace even when we're facing hard things. It doesn't matter what's happening around us, because true peace comes from within, from God's residence in our lives.

When we stay close to Him, talk to Him, and make time for Him. . .when we obey Him and try to please Him. . .He blesses us with His presence. And His presence brings peace, even when everything around us is chaos.

Thank You for Your peace, Father. I want to stay close to You and live every day in Your presence.

Day 150

The Vine

"I am the true vine, and my Father is the gardener. . . . I am the vine; you are the branches. If you remain in me and I in you, you will bear much fruit; apart from me you can do nothing."
John 15:1, 5 NIV

The key to success is surrender. Say what? You can pursue your own goals and dreams as hard as you want. But to truly succeed, it's not how hard we work for our goals—it's how well we surrender our desires and pursue what *God* wants. We can do nothing apart from Him. Anything we create or build ourselves apart from God is empty and meaningless.

To find lasting fulfillment, we need to learn the art of abiding in Christ—looking to Him for love, direction, and satisfaction. When we submit ourselves to God's way, our lives will blossom with incredible fruit. How well are you abiding in Christ? What distractions need to be pruned out of your life that are keeping you from receiving the life-giving nourishment of Jesus the Vine?

Jesus, help me remain in You today. To let go of my agenda and be in tune with Yours.

Day 151

Jesus' Friends Mary and Martha

Martha welcomed him into her house. And she had a sister called Mary, who sat at the Lord's feet and listened to his teaching.

LUKE 10:38–39 ESV

Mary and Martha were two sisters who loved Jesus and were excited to welcome Him into their home. Martha excelled at planning and preparation and probably wanted everything to be perfect for such a special guest. But Martha got upset with Mary because when Jesus arrived, Mary didn't help her with hosting and serving. Mary simply sat at Jesus' feet to listen to everything He had to say. Both sisters loved Jesus and were showing it in their own unique ways. But Jesus lovingly told Martha that Mary had chosen what was best by simply enjoying His company and listening to His teaching.

Jesus, I want to show my love for You in the details, like Martha, but I also want to choose the best way by enjoying simply being with You, like Mary. Help me to find the right balance. Amen.

Day 152

Created to Understand

You made me and formed me with your hands.
Give me understanding so I can learn your commands.
PSALM 119:73 NCV

The Lord Almighty created you with great care, love, and intention. He made you just the way you are. With His own hands He formed you.

Your Creator is for you. He specified commands to make life better for you. Sometimes His commands can seem confusing. You may not be sure you want to follow them. But instead of ignoring or forgetting His commands, ask the Lord to help you understand what He's asked you to do. Pray that He would help you learn His commands. When you ask for wisdom to better understand Him, He'll give it.

Lord, I'm in awe of You. Thank You for creating me just the way I am. I have a hard time understanding everything You'd like me to do. Would You please help me? Please show me how I can better understand You.

Day 153

Glory and Honor and Power

"You are worthy, our Lord and God, to receive glory and honor and power, for you created all things, and by your will they were created and have their being."

REVELATION 4:11 NIV

Even if it's easy to forget who you're praying to, remember that you get the privilege of praying to the God of the universe! Because of who He is, He is worthy of your glory. He's worthy of your honor. He's worthy of your praise. He created every single thing in creation. He has willed for life to exist, including your life, and He created humans in His own image. At the very least, He deserves your thanks.

One fantastic way to thank Him is to pray to Him and praise His name. You can honor Him by praying with respect and a holy fear. He is God Almighty. He is worthy of your praise.

Lord God, I praise You! You created all things, including me. You are completely powerful and so very good. I honor You.

Day 154

Tangible Ways

God showed his great love for us by sending Christ to die for us while we were still sinners.

Romans 5:8 NLT

God showed His love for you in a very tangible way through His Son's death on the cross. Even while we were stuck in a cycle of sin, God's love was burning brightly for us. So much so that He made a way to bridge the gap sin left by sacrificing Jesus. Absolutely amazing!

Today, we can choose to show love in tangible ways too. We can be the Lord's hands and feet in the world—an extension of His goodness and compassion toward others. What are some ways you can show love to those around you? How can you bless your teachers, coaches, small group leaders, friends, neighbors, and family? Ask God to help you demonstrate love in wonderful and meaningful ways, and then choose to delight each person's heart with purpose.

Lord, thank You for the tangible display of love through Jesus. Help me find tangible ways to express compassion and kindness too! Amen.

Day 155

Power to Heal

They ran throughout that whole region and carried the sick on mats to wherever they heard he was. And wherever he went—into villages, towns or countryside—they placed the sick in the marketplaces. They begged him to let them touch even the edge of his cloak, and all who touched it were healed.

MARK 6:55–56 NIV

If you or someone you care about is sick, pray. Jesus had the power in Bible times to heal people, and He still has that power today. Sometimes He doesn't heal people here on earth, but we have to remember that forever healing is promised in heaven for all who choose Jesus as the one and only Savior from their sins. There will be no more sickness or death in heaven (Revelation 21:4). Mostly, we should pray for everyone we know to choose Jesus and have forever life too.

Jesus, I pray for You to heal sickness and pain here on earth, and mostly I pray for You to heal people's hearts forever by helping them turn to You as the only Savior from their sins. Amen.

Day 156

His Plans

For I am confident of this very thing, that He who began a good work among you will complete it by the day of Christ Jesus.

PHILIPPIANS 1:6 NASB

Do you know why God created you? He thought you were a great idea. He was lonely for someone just like you. He thought you up, placed you in your mother's womb, and grew you—all because He wanted you! That's pretty incredible when you think about it.

He didn't forget about you after you were born. That was just the starting point. He wants you to choose Him, and His first big goal is to make that happen. He woos you and draws you with His love. Once you choose to have a relationship with Him, He keeps working to make you exactly who He wants you to be—which is someone amazing, special, and unique.

I choose You today, Father. I surrender to Your plans for my life. I know that Your intentions are good and that You have incredible things in store.

Day 157

King of Kings

Grace and peace to you from. . .Jesus Christ, who is the faithful witness, the firstborn from the dead, and the ruler of the kings of the earth.

REVELATION 1:4–5 NIV

Jesus is King. He rules the kings of the earth even as we wait for His return when He will permanently set up His kingdom (Revelation 19). We often think of Jesus as King only as we anticipate His coming reign, but He is still very much King today. He rules the powers of the earth with His sovereignty.

Currently, Satan is in strong opposition to Jesus' rule, and we see the epic battle of good versus evil unfold every day. No matter how badly world events decline or how strong and powerful evil becomes, you can be confident the King of Kings is ultimately in control. The world may not make sense, but you can trust Jesus' ways and timing and find safety and security in His sovereignty.

> King Jesus, sometimes the world feels out of control, but I know You are in total control. I choose to trust You and find peace and safety under Your rule.

Day 158

Loving God

"Sir, which is the most important command in the laws of Moses?" Jesus replied, "'Love the Lord your God with all your heart, soul, and mind.' This is the first and greatest commandment."

MATTHEW 22:36–38 TLB

Every day you have a choice to love God or ignore Him. You can invite Him into your hectic schedule or push through on your own. It's up to you.

How can you love the Lord with your heart, soul, and mind? Let Him be a constant companion as you navigate your day. Talk to Him about frustrating people…challenging moments…irritating situations…and discouraging news. But also share what excites you and brings joy. Tell God about your hopes and dreams. Ask for wisdom or peace when you need it. Let Him be involved in it all. When you choose to love Him in these ways, you'll be fulfilling the greatest commandment.

Lord, I'm inviting You to be part of my day, in every way. Let my heart and mind be turned toward You as I choose to love You with intentionality. Amen.

Day 159

Loving Others

"The second most important is similar:
'Love your neighbor as much as you love yourself.'"
MATTHEW 22:39 TLB

Yesterday, we learned the greatest commandment is to love God with your heart, soul, and mind. Today, we read that the second most important command is to love your neighbor (love others) in the same measure as you love yourself. While neither is easy, both are important as believers.

Loving is a choice we must make. Sometimes it's a no-brainer because certain people matter greatly to us. Even when we argue or they make us mad, our feelings for them are deep and never waver. But other times, loving feels almost impossible. It's hard to have compassion for those who have hurt you or someone you care about. When they are mean-spirited and look for ways to make you feel insignificant, how can we love?

Ask God for help. He knows every detail and will meet you in the struggle. Today, trust Him to make ways for you to choose love.

> Lord, this command feels hard, especially when it comes to certain people. Help me choose love anyway. Amen.

Day 160

Jesus Calls to Sinners Who Will Repent

Later, as Jesus left the town, he saw a tax collector named Levi sitting at his tax collector's booth. "Follow me and be my disciple," Jesus said to him. So Levi got up, left everything, and followed him. Later, Levi held a banquet in his home with Jesus as the guest of honor. Many of Levi's fellow tax collectors and other guests also ate with them. But the Pharisees and their teachers of religious law complained bitterly to Jesus' disciples, "Why do you eat and drink with such scum?" Jesus answered them, "Healthy people don't need a doctor—sick people do. I have come to call not those who think they are righteous, but those who know they are sinners and need to repent."

LUKE 5:27–32 NLT

Jesus' calling of Levi shows us that people who know they are sinners will choose to follow Jesus. Those who think they do not need forgiveness will not see their need of Him.

Jesus, I know I'm a sinner, and I need Your grace and forgiveness. Thank You for giving it so generously.

Day 161

Rescue Story

I call upon the L*ORD*, *who is worthy to be praised,*
and I am saved from my enemies.
PSALM 18:3 NASB

David wrote this psalm on the day God rescued him from people who wanted to kill him. David hadn't done anything to deserve this treatment. He didn't lash out at God and say, "Why would You let me go through this?" He knew that other people are going to make bad choices that affect us. He also knew that God was his only hope of escape.

Are you dealing with others' bad choices right now? Do you feel like your problems are more than you can handle? God is bigger. Call out to Him like David did. Praise Him for His love, His power, and His goodness. Praise Him for rescuing you—even before the rescue happens. God loves you more than anything, and you are His first priority.

You know what I'm facing, Father. Please rescue me soon. I praise You because I know You're working right now.

Day 162

Our High Priest

My friends, the blood of Jesus gives us courage to enter the most holy place by a new way that leads to life! And this way takes us through the curtain that is Christ himself. We have a great high priest who is in charge of God's house. So let's come near God with pure hearts and a confidence that comes from having faith. Let's keep our hearts pure, our consciences free from evil, and our bodies washed with clean water.

HEBREWS 10:19–22 CEV

In the Old Testament, God's physical presence dwelled inside the temple in a section called the Most Holy Place. A curtain separated the Most Holy Place from the Holy Place (Exodus 26:33). Only the high priest was allowed in the Most Holy Place—and only once a year on the Day of Atonement (Leviticus 16). When Jesus died, the curtain in the temple ripped in two (Matthew 27:51). We are no longer separated from God's presence! You can confidently approach Him about *anything*.

Jesus, thank You for being my High Priest so I can always be in Your presence.

Day 163

Gracious Protection

Then the LORD God provided a leafy plant and made it grow up over Jonah to give shade for his head to ease his discomfort, and Jonah was very happy about the plant.
JONAH 4:6 NIV

The story of Jonah gives us a picture of God's overwhelming grace. God instructed Jonah to tell the people of Nineveh to turn from their sin. Rather than obey God's command, Jonah fled. During Jonah's disobedience, God provided a plant to grow for his comfort and protection. When Jonah finally obeyed, the Ninevites listened, repented, and were spared God's judgment.

The Lord protects us even in our rebellion. This is not an excuse to keep running from obedience but an opportunity to praise God for His mercy. If you're basking in God-given comforts while avoiding what God's calling you to do, don't delay any longer! Listen, obey, and watch God work!

Dear God, I'm sorry for ignoring Your voice.
I know obedience brings peace and joy.
Help me do what I know You're calling me to do!

Day 164

Wow!

I look at your heavens, which you made with your fingers. I see the moon and stars, which you created. But why are people even important to you? Why do you take care of human beings?

Psalm 8:3–4 NCV

Look outside. In fact, if it's possible, get up, go outside, and look up. What do you see? Whether it's day or night, look up at the heavens. God made them with His fingers. He made the moon. He made the stars. He made the sun. He made the clouds. Everything amazing you see? God made it all. Consider the beauty of creation, and then consider that the God who created the heavens and the earth also created you.

Because of the way He not only created you but also cares for you every single day, it's time to thank Him. Praise Him for the way He cares just for you.

> Lord, You are amazing! I can't even imagine how You've created everything, but I'm so grateful that You have—and that You care for everything too.

Day 165

The Best Influencer

We can be sure that we know Him if we obey His teaching. Anyone who says, "I know Him," but does not obey His teaching is a liar. There is no truth in him. But whoever obeys His Word has the love of God made perfect in him. This is the way to know if you belong to Christ. The one who says he belongs to Christ should live the same kind of life Christ lived.

1 John 2:3–6 NLV

You might be impressed by and look up to certain celebrities and influencers, but be sure to choose Jesus as your number one role model. God the Father sent His Son, Jesus Christ, to earth to be a human being just like all of us and to be our example for living the best kind of life. And how we do follow His example? By reading and studying God's Word to learn more about who God is and how Jesus lived. And by keeping in close relationship with Jesus through prayer and worship.

Jesus, You are my very best influencer and role model. Please help me love learning about You and keep me growing closer to You. Amen.

Day 166

He Is for Me

From my distress I called upon the LORD*; the* LORD *answered me and put me in an open space. The Lord is for me; I will not fear; what can man do to me? The* LORD *is for me among those who help me; therefore I will look with satisfaction on those who hate me.*

PSALM 118:5–7 NASB

It's easy to focus on people who don't like us. The mean ones. The bullies. But God doesn't want us to put so much attention on them that we forget who our Father is. He's not just powerful. He's *all-powerful.* And He's fierce when it comes to defending His own.

If a person or a group is making your life hard, do what you must to remain safe. Talk to a parent, teacher, or counselor. But don't let your enemies steal your peace. God is with you, He's on your side, and He will take care of you.

> You know what I'm going through, Father. Give me wisdom for how to respond. I trust You, and I know You'll take care of me.

Day 167

Treasure Hunt

"The kingdom of heaven is like treasure hidden in a field. When a man found it, he hid it again, and then in his joy went and sold all he had and bought that field."

MATTHEW 13:44 NIV

Jesus shared a powerful truth about the kingdom of heaven in this simple story. The truth of who Jesus is (John 3:16), what He's rescued us from (Luke 16:22–24), and what He offers us for eternity (1 Peter 1:3–5) is such a profound treasure that it should flood us with joy and cause us to voluntarily give up *everything* to possess it.

Jesus Christ and His kingdom are treasures of incomparable worth. He surpasses anything we could pursue in this world. Do you see Jesus as that treasure? Are you pursuing Him passionately above everything else? Or is He just kinda worth your time? If you just sorta dabble with Christian activities, you don't yet fully understand the treasure Jesus is and offers. Keep digging deeper until you find it!

Jesus, help me recognize the treasure You are and value You enough that I'd give up everything in a heartbeat for You.

Day 168

Being Patient with Others

Be humble and gentle. Be patient with each other, making allowance for each other's faults because of your love. Try always to be led along together by the Holy Spirit and so be at peace with one another.

Ephesians 4:2–3 TLB

When we are patient with others, it's an act of love. Every time we refuse to sit in judgment when they fail, we are loving them. God wants us to live peacefully with those around us, and we can't make that happen if we're critical. We can't be reckless with how we treat others. Instead, the Lord tells us to be humble and gentle.

Community is important to God, and He wants us to handle one another with care. His plan is for peace. So ask Him to help you be full of kindness and compassion, especially when you're struggling to be that way. Ask for perspective so you can choose love even when it's difficult. And trust God to align your heart for others with His.

Lord, help me choose to love others well by being patient, humble, and gentle. Amen.

Day 169

A Blessed Prayer

Now Jabez called on the God of Israel, saying, "Oh that You would greatly bless me and extend my border, and that Your hand might be with me, and that You would keep me from harm so that it would not hurt me!" And God brought about what he requested.

1 Chronicles 4:10 NASB

Have you ever done a genealogy test? The kind where they track where you and your family came from? In the Bible, 1 Chronicles reads like a big family tree. Descendants of Israel are listed, with little or no information given about each person. That changes, though, when we get to Jabez. The writer stops to tell us something important about Jabez: he asked something of God, and God gave it to him.

Jabez loved the Lord and trusted God enough to ask for blessings. We serve a God who delights in being asked for things by His children. God will only do what's best for us, which frees us to ask big and leave the outcome in His hands.

Lord, Your blessings are incredible! I ask that You always be near, help me succeed, and protect me from harm.

Day 170

Jesus Heals a Blind Man

As he went along, he saw a man blind from birth. His disciples asked him, "Rabbi, who sinned, this man or his parents, that he was born blind?" "Neither this man nor his parents sinned," said Jesus, "but this happened so that the works of God might be displayed in him. As long as it is day, we must do the works of him who sent me. Night is coming, when no one can work. While I am in the world, I am the light of the world." After saying this, he spit on the ground, made some mud with the saliva, and put it on the man's eyes. "Go," he told him, "wash in the Pool of Siloam." . . . So the man went and washed, and came home seeing.

JOHN 9:1–7 NIV

Jesus taught that this man was born blind so that God's work could be shown in him when Jesus healed him and restored his sight. This helps us know that whatever we're struggling with, we can let God's will and work be done and pray for His glory to be shown.

Jesus, thank You for Your healing power. I praise You and want all people to see Your glory! Amen.

Day 171

Money

Keep your lives free from the love of money and be content with what you have, because God has said, "Never will I leave you; never will I forsake you."
HEBREWS 13:5 NIV

This verse is often misunderstood. So is 1 Timothy 6:10 (NIV), which states, "The love of money is a root of all kinds of evil." God never says money is bad. He always supplies what we need, and sometimes that's money.

Money isn't evil. It's not good either. It's just paper and metal. It can't think or make decisions. The *love* of money, however, can pull us away from God and destroy our lives. Ask God to help you be happy with what you have, whether it's a little or a lot. He will never leave you and, really, He is all you need.

Thank You for giving me everything I need, Father. Help me be content with what I have instead of always focusing on money and the things it can buy. I love You, and You're all I need.

Day 172

What Do You Say?

When Jesus came to the region of Caesarea Philippi, he asked his disciples, "Who do people say the Son of Man is?" They replied, "Some say John the Baptist; others say Elijah; and still others, Jeremiah or one of the prophets." "But what about you?" he asked. "Who do you say I am?" Simon Peter answered, "You are the Messiah, the Son of the living God."

MATTHEW 16:13–16 NIV

This was a defining moment for the disciples. They had witnessed Jesus' miracles. Heard His teaching. Followed Him for some time now. Through a series of questions, Jesus led them to a moment of clarity when they professed their faith in Him for the first time.

People today offer the same answers about Jesus. Many declare that Jesus was a great teacher or a prophet or an influential religious man who encouraged peace and love. Or they simply say He was a good person. But the piercing question is "Who do *you* say Jesus is?" Have you experienced that life-defining realization and declaration like the disciples?

Lord, I know this is the most important question I will ever answer. I say You are. . .

Day 173

So Happy You Could Sing

David sang this song to the LORD when the LORD saved him from Saul and all his other enemies. He said: "The LORD is my rock, my fortress, my Savior. My God is my rock. I can run to him for safety. He is my shield and my saving strength, my defender and my place of safety. . . . I will call to the LORD, who is worthy of praise, and I will be saved from my enemies."

2 SAMUEL 22:1–4 NCV

Think about a time when you couldn't help but sing. There's something about music that you just can't keep inside. The same can be said about happiness or joy—you can't keep all the good feelings to yourself.

Just like David sang when he had a huge victory, you can sing to the Lord. When you know God has answered your prayers, thank Him! Praise the Lord when you're happy! Sing to Him when He brings relief. Create a song that reminds you of all the wonderful things He's done.

Lord, You're my rock and fortress. I can run to You for safety. You're my strength and shield. You're my defender and my safe place. You're worthy of my praise!

Day 174

Loving Through Obedience

"If you love me, show it by doing what I've told you. I will talk to the Father, and he'll provide you another Friend so that you will always have someone with you. This Friend is the Spirit of Truth."

John 14:15 MSG

When we obey God, it reveals our heart. Choosing to do what He asks shows that we love Him over our own fleshly desires. Just like it does for our parents, following His rules speaks volumes by showing we care about what's important. And it's honoring.

While we may try, obeying often takes divine intervention. Our humanity kicks in and we get rebellious from time to time. We want to do things our own way and on our own timeline. And because God knew our needs, He sent the Holy Spirit. As our friend, He's the one who enables us to obey. The Spirit is a constant companion who will always bring truth. And with His help, we can choose to love God through obedience.

Lord, thank You for the Holy Spirit, who empowers me to love You through obedience. Amen.

Day 175

Leave Grudges Behind

Make a clean break with all cutting, backbiting, profane talk. Be gentle with one another, sensitive. Forgive one another as quickly and thoroughly as God in Christ forgave you.

Ephesians 4:31–32 MSG

Have you ever done something that you wish you could go back and undo? Now, what if someone brought up that "something" every time they saw you? Think of the shame and embarrassment you'd feel if you were constantly reminded of your mistake.

One of the kindest things you can do for someone is forgive quickly and not weaponize their past sins—especially if they're doing their best to learn and grow from them. We all make mistakes. When someone does something hurtful, handle it with gentleness, and don't bring up flaws as a way of punishing them.

Holy Spirit, please convict me when I'm about to use the past unfairly against someone. Help me forgive fully and always be gentle.

Day 176

The God of Miracles

On the day that the Lord *gave up the Amorites to the Israelites, Joshua stood before all the people of Israel and said to the* Lord*: "Sun, stand still over Gibeon. Moon, stand still over the Valley of Aijalon." So the sun stood still, and the moon stopped until the people defeated their enemies. . . . The sun stopped in the middle of the sky and waited to go down for a full day.*

Joshua 10:12–13 NCV

God is a God of miracles. And once when the Israelites were in battle, their leader, Joshua, prayed for the sun and moon to stand still until they were victorious. God not only brought a victory for the Israelites, but He also stopped the sun and moon in their places for a full day.

You may never witness a miracle like the sun stopping, but you can remember that the God you pray to is the God of miracles.

Lord God, You are absolutely amazing!
I'm so grateful I can come to You at any time.
No prayer request is too big for You!

Day 177

Work Hard for Jesus

Do not be lazy but always work hard.
Work for the Lord with a heart full of love for Him.
ROMANS 12:11 NLV

What is your work ethic like? Are you willing to work hard? Do you do your best with the gifts and talents God has given you? Having a good work ethic doesn't mean you should never rest or have fun—you absolutely should! But it's so easy to become lazy and have too much rest and fun. Think of the Lord Jesus Himself as the boss overseeing you in any task you do, because ultimately He is! But He's the best kind of boss—full of love and blessing for you as you do the good work you were created for (see Ephesians 2:10).

Jesus, I want to have a work ethic that shows others I work to honor You most of all. Please help me give my best effort and find joy in my work, no matter what it is. You are so good to me, and I'm honored to do my best for You! Amen.

Day 178

Give Thanks

Give thanks in all circumstances;
for this is God's will for you in Christ Jesus.
1 Thessalonians 5:18 NIV

Mental health researchers have discovered overwhelming evidence that doing one thing makes a huge difference in how happy we are. That thing is gratitude. People who make a point to be grateful for the things they have instead of focusing on what they don't have or don't like are happier.

It didn't take scientific research to uncover this truth. It's right here in God's Word! No matter how bad things get, we can always find something to be thankful for. God wants us to give thanks in all circumstances. This will lead us to the peace and joy He desires for us.

It's easy to focus on the things I don't like about my life, Father. But when I focus on the things I'm grateful for, the list keeps growing. Thank You for ______. Thank You for loving me. Thank You for my salvation and for Your Son, Jesus Christ.

Day 179

New Identity

This means that anyone who belongs to Christ has become a new person. The old life is gone; a new life has begun!
2 Corinthians 5:17 NLT

When we ask Jesus to forgive our sins and we surrender our lives to Him, we begin a new life. God cleanses us and restores us spiritually. We go from spiritually dead in our sins to spiritually resurrected and alive! We are a new person—and we have a new identity.

Our old identities have lived with us so long they can feel permanently attached to us. Our old identities speak lies and destroy our confidence: "I don't belong. I'm unlovable. I'm not good enough." But you have a new identity in Christ! Recognizing and understanding who you are in Christ will give you the confidence and security you need.

What old identity still creeps around your thoughts? What do you believe about yourself—and does that match with who Christ says you are? That old life has gone! Step into your new identity, and let the truth of who you are in Christ give you assurance and freedom!

Lord, help me understand who I am in You and embrace my new identity.

Day 180

Seek Him First

"But seek first his kingdom and his righteousness, and all these things will be given to you as well."
MATTHEW 6:33 NIV

Right before this verse, Jesus told His listeners not to worry about what they'll eat or drink or wear. He reminds them that God feeds the birds and clothes the flowers in beautiful splendor. And we mean a whole lot more to God than birds or flowers.

Don't waste a single minute worrying about the necessities of life. Instead of worrying, pray! Seek God. Tell Him what you need. Live to please Him, and He will bless you in the most unexpected ways. A cousin might show up with a bag of designer clothes she doesn't want anymore. A neighbor might bring a casserole because she made too much. Make God your first priority, and He will take care of every single need.

Father, You know the things I want and the things I need. More than anything, I want to be close to You. I trust You with all the rest.

Day 181

Leading and Guiding

Send me your light and truth to guide me.
Let them lead me to your holy mountain, to where you live.
Psalm 43:3 NCV

Life can be confusing. Some days, it might feel like you're in the dark and have no idea which way to turn. Other days, you realize you need to make a decision from so many different choices, and you have no clue what's best.

When you have no idea what to do or decide, don't try to figure things out on your own. Don't even talk over all your options again and again with your best friend. Stop yourself and pray. Ask God to guide you. Ask Him to lead you and make your way clear. He'll send His light and His truth to guide you. He'll lead you, but you need to ask Him first.

Father, help me remember to ask You first! When I'm confused, please guide me. When I don't know what choice to make, please lead me to the right decision.

Day 182

The Gift of True Friends

A friend is always loyal, and a brother is born to help in time of need.
Proverbs 17:17 NLT

What a gift to be a true friend and to have a true friend. Sometimes they are the ones we lean on the most to walk us through the hard times. They're often our secret keepers, heart protectors, problem solvers, and soul sisters. And we know we can depend on their love and kindness, regardless of the situation we find ourselves wading through.

Who are your true friends? Who are you a true friend for? Take a moment to thank God for these gifts, as scripture says all good things come from above. Because He loves you, these kinds of friends have been handpicked. Some for this season and others for a lifetime. But they make a difference in our lives in deep and meaningful ways.

If you don't have them yet, pray them into your life! Tell God your need and wait for Him to bring them at the right time.

Lord, thank You for the gift of true friends. Help me be one too! Amen.

Day 183

A Soft Answer

A gentle response defuses anger,
but a sharp tongue kindles a temper-fire.
PROVERBS 15:1 MSG

When it comes to handling fire, certain substances will extinguish a flame, while other things will cause it to grow. When it comes to emotions, certain responses will put out anger, while other responses will feed it.

As fires grow, they get even harder to put out. A sarcastic, angry, or passive-aggressive response will only escalate things. A gentle response, however, is like throwing a bucket of cold water on a fire. It'll stall its growth or put it out entirely.

> Dear God, I know it's best to always respond with gentleness, but sometimes it's so hard not to get defensive. I'm going to work on extinguishing anger before it spreads.

Day 184

Give with Great Faith

A poor woman whose husband had died came by and gave two very small pieces of money.

MARK 12:42 NLV

One day, Jesus watched many rich people give large offerings to God at the temple. Giving a lot wasn't hard for them because they were so rich that they had plenty of money to share. But then, Jesus watched one woman who was very poor and had no husband drop in two coins that were worth less than one cent. And Jesus said to His disciples, "This poor widow has given more money than all the others." But how was that possible? Jesus said, "The rich people put in money they didn't even need because they have so much extra. But the poor widow has nothing extra. She needed every bit of her money to live on, but still she gave it all to God."

Jesus, I want to give to You with great faith just like this widow did, because I trust that You will provide for me no matter what and that Your blessings are greater than anything I could ever gain on my own. Amen.

Day 185

Delight in Him

Take delight in the L*ORD, and he will give you the desires of your heart.*

Psalm 37:4 NIV

What are your secret dreams and wishes? What are your goals? All those desires that live inside your heart. . .God already knows about them. He created you, and He knows what will make you happy. He knows what will lead you to a fulfilled, satisfying life. That's what He wants for you—to live out the purpose He had in mind when He created you.

When we delight in God—when we get excited about talking to Him, seek His advice about everything, and try to make Him happy—our desires naturally fall in line with what He wants for us. He delights in giving us the desires of our hearts when we delight in Him.

Teach me what it means to delight in You, Father. You are my everything, and I love You with all my heart. Take my dreams, give them wings, and let me live in a way that glorifies You.

Day 186

Child of God

But to all who believed him and accepted him,
he gave the right to become children of God.
John 1:12 NLT

You are a child of God. If you have confessed your sins and accepted Jesus' gift of salvation, you are God's daughter! He's adopted you into His family! "I will be your Father, and you will be my sons and daughters, says the Lord Almighty" (2 Corinthians 6:18 NLT). And since we are His daughters, God has made us His heirs (Galatians 4:7). We will inherit His kingdom (James 2:5), and we have assurance that we will inherit eternal life (Titus 3:7).

You have a place in God's family. You are wanted and accepted. You have purpose and value. The world constantly tells you that you are not enough, but in God's sight, you are everything. Hold your head high and face today with confidence. You're a daughter of the King!

Father, thank You for adopting me into Your family. When the world tries to tell me I'm worthless, help me remember how much You love me and how much value I have in Your eyes.

Day 187

Cautious Anger

Be not quick in your spirit to become angry,
for anger lodges in the heart of fools.
Ecclesiastes 7:9 esv

If you want to see the worst of humanity, go to a popular YouTube video and read the comments. They're filled with hurtful, hateful, and angry remarks, often having nothing to do with the video they're under.

We live in a society that's incredibly quick to become angry and offended over the smallest things. It's not enough to quietly dislike or disagree with someone; many people feel the need to completely tear the person down.

Rather than give yourself over to anger, try to become "unoffendable." Be the kind of person others can talk to without fearing an angry outburst or condescending lecture. If you must express an opinion or speak a truth, say it with gentleness and love, listening as much as you talk. (Oh, and try to do it face-to-face, not Facebook-to-Facebook. That always goes much better.)

Dear Jesus, I know it's important to be slow to anger. Make me someone who stays calm even when everyone else is worked up.

Day 188

How to Pray

Jesus said to them, "When you pray, say: 'Father, may your name always be kept holy. May your kingdom come. Give us the food we need for each day. Forgive us for our sins, because we forgive everyone who has done wrong to us. And do not cause us to be tempted.'"

LUKE 11:2–4 NCV

During His time on earth, Jesus taught others how to pray, so there's no need for guessing what to say. As Jesus taught, our prayers need to acknowledge God's holiness. He's worthy of our praise. We should ask Him to bring His kingdom here to earth, and for our daily food.

Asking for forgiveness and asking for the ability to forgive others are both important requests to remember. Finally, you can ask for God to help you stand strong against temptation. As you pray like Jesus modeled, you can cover all the necessary areas of your life.

Father, may Your name be kept holy. May Your kingdom come. Please give me food I need today. Please forgive my sins. Help me forgive others, and protect me from temptation.

Day 189

You Are His Child

See how very much our heavenly Father loves us,
for he allows us to be called his children—think of it—
and we really are! But since most people don't know God,
naturally they don't understand that we are his children.

1 John 3:1 TLB

God chose you! Out of His great love, the Lord has fully embraced you as His child. Even with all your flaws—with every shortcoming and imperfection—you're allowed to be called a child of the Most High. Regardless of the ugly moments when you screamed at your siblings, were rude to your parents, or betrayed a friend, you are deeply loved. And there is nothing that can change it.

Friend, you have the ability to choose God every day too. A *yes* to spending time in prayer, reading His Word, meditating on scripture, listening to a sermon, or soaking in worship music allows you to reciprocate His love in meaningful ways. The intentionality of those decisions delights God's heart. They speak loudly about your faith. And they draw you closer to the Father.

Lord, I love being called Your child.
Help me love You back! Amen.

Day 190

Love God, Not Money

Don't love money; be satisfied with what you have. For God has said, "I will never fail you. I will never abandon you."

Hebrews 13:5 NLT

Money can get you a lot in life: comfort, status, education, access to health care, trendy clothes, and lots of material possessions. Money, however, can't buy some of the most important things you need. A large bank account will never heal your broken heart or forgive your sin. It will never bring you peace of mind. (After all, the more you have, the more you have to lose.) Wealth won't give you more friends (at least not true friends), a better attitude, or fulfillment. In fact, a love for money often overshadows a love for kindness.

Don't obsess over getting temporary, perishable things. Instead, develop a love for God, who stores up irreplaceable treasures for you in heaven. Be grateful for the provision God's given you, be it great or small, and give thanks that the most important things you need were given freely on the cross.

Lord, I know money was given to be used for Your glory. Help keep me from getting attached to money and earthly things.

Day 191

He Came to Care for Others

"The Son of Man came not to be cared for. He came to care for others. He came to give His life so that many could be bought by His blood and made free from the punishment of sin."
MATTHEW 20:28 NLV

Jesus is called the Son of Man, and He is King of all kings and Lord of all lords. But He definitely didn't come to earth in the way we would normally think of royalty—important people who have fancy, expensive everything and servants and staff waiting on their every need. No, Jesus came as a regular person to serve and care for *us*. He cared so much that He even gave His life for us to save us from sin. And once we trust Him as Savior, He asks us to imitate Him by serving and caring for others so that they will want to know Him as Savior too.

Jesus, You are the very best example of loving and serving others. I want to be as much like You as I possibly can! Amen.

Day 192

For My Good

And we know that in all things God works for the good of those who love him, who have been called according to his purpose.

Romans 8:28 NIV

We've all heard someone say, "It will work out for the best." That's a true statement, sort of. If we ignore God and do whatever we want, not caring about the consequences to ourselves or others, we'll probably end up in jail. But if we love God with our whole hearts and choose to follow Him and obey His Word, if we do our best to live out His divine purpose for our lives—to love God and love other people—God will make sure things work out for our good. Even if we end up in jail for serving Him, we'll be in good company because He will never leave us.

I love You with my whole heart, Father. I trust Your plans for me, and I know that even when things seem bad, You're working everything out for my good. I trust You completely.

Day 193

Called by Name

"Do not be afraid, for I have ransomed you.
I have called you by name; you are mine."
ISAIAH 43:1 NLT

God knows your name. Who's your favorite celeb? Imagine going to an event where they'll be. You're jammed into the tight crowd of fans, but the celeb turns, looks straight at you, and calls your name. How floored would you be that this celebrity *knows your name*?!

God, the Creator and Sustainer of the universe, knows *your* name. He's called you out of the masses of humanity and claimed you as His own. He paid your ransom for sin, and you are His. God is not some "Man Upstairs" who's so busy running the world that He doesn't notice you or care about you. He is a strong Father who unconditionally loves you. He sees you and knows your name. He will do anything to save you and protect you.

How does the truth that God claims you give you reassurance today?

God, I'm so humbled that You've ransomed me and called me by name. I have incredible worth and value to You. May this truth sink deep into my heart and give me confidence today.

Day 194

Jesus Can Make Our Weak Faith Stronger

"Lord, I have faith. Help my weak faith to be stronger!"
MARK 9:24 NLV

A father was asking Jesus for help for his son, and it was so hard for the man to imagine that Jesus could do what he was asking. The father said to Jesus, "Have mercy on us and help us, if you can." Jesus replied, "What do you mean, 'If I can'? . . . Anything is possible if a person believes" (Mark 9:22–23 NLT). And the father said, "Lord, I have faith. Help my weak faith to be stronger!"

When we pray, we have to remember that Jesus is able to do exactly what we ask and so much more! He may or may not answer the way we hope, but no matter how He responds to our prayers, our main response should be "Lord, I have faith. Help my weak faith be stronger!"

Jesus, please make my faith in You stronger and stronger every day! Amen.

Day 195

Biblical Revenge

If your enemy is hungry, give him food to eat; if he is thirsty, give him water to drink. In doing this, you will heap burning coals on his head, and the LORD will reward you.

PROVERBS 25:21–22 NIV

Did you know that kindness can be used as a weapon against your enemy? If you want to get revenge on someone who's hurt you, treat them kindly.

Goodness catches wicked people off guard. When someone mistreats you, they expect anger and retaliation. (Two normal responses when hurt.) If that doesn't happen, it confuses them or even angers them. Meeting anger with kindness shows your enemy that their actions didn't shake your foundation.

By offering blessings instead of curses, you show your enemy that there's another way. In fact, your generous reaction might even convict them of their sin and make them rethink the path they're on. No matter their response, the Lord will see your obedience and reward you.

Father God, it's so hard to show kindness to the people who make my life miserable. Give me the strength to be kind even when I want revenge.

Day 196

Seen

She gave this name to the LORD who spoke to her: "You are the God who sees me," for she said, "I have now seen the One who sees me."

GENESIS 16:13 NIV

In Genesis, we can read about the story of Hagar, a pregnant woman who was running away from her problems. Nothing in her life seemed ideal. And as she found herself alone, she debated what she would do next. The angel of the Lord came and talked with Hagar, filling her with encouragement and hope. When their conversation was over, Hagar knew that God saw her.

He was the God who saw Hagar, and He is the God who sees you.

When you feel alone or find yourself in a situation you never imagined, remember God is the God who sees you. He sees you, He hears you, He knows you, and He loves you.

Father, You are the God who sees me. Thank You that I'm never alone!

Day 197

Never Forsaken

Those who know your name trust in you, for you, Lord, have never forsaken those who seek you.

Psalm 9:10 NIV

God promises to never forsake us. To forsake means to abandon, leave behind, or turn your back on something. It also means to give up on, reject, or disown. You can't really forsake a person you don't even know. But if you turn your back on a close friend, that's hurtful.

The first step to God's total and complete loyalty is to know Him and trust Him. Romans 10:13 tells us that everyone who calls on the Lord's name will be saved. If you want to be part of His family, tell Him so! He will accept you with open arms, and you can trust He will always, always have your back.

I trust You alone, God, for everything I need. Thank You for always being my biggest fan and my best friend. I love You with all my heart.

Day 198

Unconditionally Loved

I am sure that nothing can separate us from God's love—
not life or death, not angels or spirits, not the present or the future,
and not powers above or powers below. Nothing in all creation
can separate us from God's love for us in Christ Jesus our Lord!
ROMANS 8:38–39 CEV

You are loved. Unconditionally. Completely. Just as you are.

Do you truly believe that? Nothing you've done in the past—or will do in the future—changes God's love for you. Nothing that's been done to you changes God's love for you. None of your failures and flaws change God's love for you. He *loves* you. Take a minute to really soak in the enormity of this love. Let love comfort you, heal broken places inside you, and give you confidence as you face this day.

Loving Father, thank You for Your amazing love! You always accept me, always have time for me, always want to be with me, and always love me—no matter what. Help me truly grasp how much You love me. May Your love heal my broken and hurting places inside.

Day 199

He Knows

You have recorded my troubles. You have kept a list of my tears. Aren't they in your records?

Psalm 56:8 NCV

You're never alone. Even on your worst, most heartbroken days, the Lord is there. He knows all the troubles you have, and He pays attention to every single tear you cry. While sadness is part of this life, you're not alone when you face hard times. The Lord pays attention to all of your anger, all of your grief, all of your confusion.

Because God sees and knows, you don't have to spend time explaining details to Him. He understands. You can just pour out your feelings and tell Him what you're thinking. Be completely honest and trust that your feelings are meaningful not just to you but also to your heavenly Father.

> Father, I wish I didn't have to go through hard times. But since I do, I'm so grateful I'm not going through them alone. I am relieved that You're always there, and You always know.

Day 200

Seeing the Fruit

So if we stay close to him, obedient to him, we won't be sinning either; but as for those who keep on sinning, they should realize this: They sin because they have never really known him or become his.

1 John 3:6 TLB

This scripture is a very strong warning for everyone who calls themselves a believer. When we accept Jesus as God's Son and our personal Savior, there should be a heart transformation. Our lives should look and feel different. We should want to abandon our old self—our sinful and selfish ways—and instead embrace a new life in Christ.

As we stay close to God and obey the commands we find in the Bible, recognize this decision is a beautiful act of love. We're choosing to grow in our faith by following Him. What God finds important, we do too. What He wants for our lives, we do as well. But if instead we aren't changing our focus from self to Savior, let it be a red flag. Did we really choose to love God with our whole heart?

Lord, let me see the fruit that comes from a genuine relationship with You. Amen.

Day 201

Lost and Found

"This younger son. . .wasted all his money in wild living."
Luke 15:13 NLT

Jesus taught about a son who took all of his inheritance from his father and spent it all on a wild and crazy life. After all his money was gone, he was hungry and alone, and the only job he could find was feeding pigs. Then he was ashamed of himself, so he got up and started for home. While he was still a long way off, his father saw him and felt full of love and kindness toward him. He ran to his son and threw his arms around him. The son said, "Father, I have sinned against both heaven and you, and I am no longer worthy of being called your son" (Luke 15:18–19 NLT). But the father said to his workmen, "We must celebrate with a feast, for this son of mine was dead and has now returned to life. He was lost, but now he is found" (Luke 15:23–24 NLT).

Jesus, like You taught in this parable, help me to realize my mistakes, own them, apologize for them, and turn away from them and back to Your good ways. Thank You for Your love and mercy. Amen.

Day 202

Choosing Friends

But Jesus would not entrust himself to them, for he knew all people.

John 2:24 NIV

In this passage, Jesus had worked a lot of miracles, and people thought He was a superstar. But He knew better than to trust their loyalty because He knew how people operate. They were impressed now because He was doing some really cool stuff. But what about tomorrow? What about when He moved to the next town? He knew their devotion would weaken.

God wants us to be wise about who we trust. It's great to enjoy someone's offer of friendship, but don't share all your secrets or give too much of yourself away until you can be certain of their loyalty. Instead, love them but ask God to give you wisdom about who to bring into your "inner circle" of trusted, best friends.

Everyone needs friends, Lord. Sometimes I choose the wrong friends, and they end up betraying me. I know I should treat everyone with love and respect. But give me wisdom about who to make my close friends.

Day 203

Fully Forgiven

He has removed our sins as far from us as the east is from the west.

Psalm 103:12 NLT

You are forgiven. God's forgiveness is different than human forgiveness. In our human nature, we might forgive, but we don't forget. God? His forgiveness deletes our sin forever. East and west never intersect. If you head east, you can continue heading east forever. If you head west, you can travel west forever. That's how far God has removed your sin: it's forever separated from you.

Not only has God completely removed your sin, but He "remembers your sins no more" (Isaiah 43:25 NIV). So when you confess and ask God to forgive your sins, they're gone! Shame has no place in your life. Guilt has no place in your life. God doesn't remember your sin, so you can forget about it too. Live free and confident in the amazing gift of forgiveness God gives us!

Amazing Father, Your gift of forgiveness is astounding. Thank You for forgiving me. Help me let go of guilt and shame and live confidently in Your forgiveness.

Day 204

Talking with God

Now when Abram was ninety-nine years old, the Lord appeared to Abram and said to him, "I am God Almighty; walk before Me, and be blameless. I will make My covenant between Me and you, and I will multiply you exceedingly." Abram fell on his face, and God talked with him.

Genesis 17:1–3 NASB

Abram was an ordinary man who experienced something extraordinary when he was old. God appeared to him and talked with him. This was not an everyday occurrence. In fact, Abram fell on his face when he experienced this.

Out of everyone, God chose Abram. He chose to make a specific promise with him, and He chose to talk with him. Even though you're not Abram, you can still follow God's requests for Abram. You can choose to walk before God. You can try to be blameless. Yes, everyone sins, but there's a big difference between willfully choosing to sin and trying to live a life that's blameless. You also can choose to talk with God through prayer.

God Almighty, You are holy! I want to walk before You and know You more!

Day 205

Examination Time

Examine me, Lord, and put me to the test; refine my mind and my heart. For Your goodness is before my eyes, and I have walked in Your truth.

Psalm 26:2–3 NASB

It can be so easy to think that no one sees what you're doing or no one knows what you're thinking. So when the psalmist asks God to examine him and put him to the test, it can seem scary. Ask God to examine me? Put me to the test?

The thing is, God already knows. When He examines you, don't think about the ways He sees all you're doing wrong. Don't worry if He notices all the things you "should" be doing. Instead, ask Him to examine you so that your mind and your heart can improve. Asking God to change you will only make you better. Put His goodness before you in what you see and say and do, and you won't have to worry about any examination.

Lord, You know me. You know my heart and my mind. Examine me so I can walk in Your truth.

Day 206

Showing Love

So now we can tell who is a child of God and who belongs to Satan. Whoever is living a life of sin and doesn't love his brother shows that he is not in God's family; for the message to us from the beginning has been that we should love one another.

1 John 3:10–11 TLB

When you choose to hold on to unforgiveness rather than choose to love others, it is telling. Each time we hold a grudge against a friend, refuse to forgive a parent, hate a teacher or coach, stay angry at a sibling, or let offenses rule our day, it reveals the state of our heart. The Lord is crystal clear in His command to love one another. As a matter of fact, it's the second-greatest command He makes.

Let's be women who choose to love, even when it takes all we have. Let's decide that nothing trumps God's charge to show care and compassion to those around us. And let's remember that selfishness is a sin. With His help, we can learn to embrace His will over our own. We can choose to love.

Lord, help me show love. . .always. Amen.

Day 207

Physically and Spiritually

[Jesus said:] "Is it easier to say to the paralyzed man 'Your sins are forgiven,' or 'Stand up, pick up your mat, and walk'? So I will prove to you that the Son of Man has the authority on earth to forgive sins." Then Jesus turned to the paralyzed man and said, "Stand up, pick up your mat, and go home!" And the man jumped up, grabbed his mat, and walked out through the stunned onlookers. They were all amazed and praised God, exclaiming, "We've never seen anything like this before!"

MARK 2:9–12 NLT

Read this whole account in Mark 2, and you'll see that this paralyzed man had been lowered into the room where Jesus was through a hole in the roof! There were so many people crowded in to listen to Jesus teach that day that there was no other way to reach Him. Jesus was impressed by their faith, and through this experience, He taught those listening that He has the power to heal both physically and spiritually. Only the one true God can forgive sins, and Jesus was proving that He is one with God.

Jesus, Your power, authority, mercy, and love are amazing! Amen.

Day 208

Your Word

This is my comfort in my misery, that Your word has revived me.
Psalm 119:50 NASB

King David, the author of this psalm, had everything a man could ever want. But he experienced some pretty awful times too. When he was young, after killing Goliath and saving Israel, the man who was king then, King Saul, got jealous and tried to kill David. Poor David had to hide in caves and beg for food just to survive. Later, David made some bad choices that hurt a lot of people. Then he watched his son get sick and die.

Whether his hard times were his own fault or because of something out of his control, David knew where to find comfort: God's Word. Hebrews 4:12 tells us that the Word of God is a living thing. When we spend time reading what God says, it changes us, comforts us, and gives us new life.

You know all the things that make me miserable right now, Lord. Thank You for Your Word. Remind me to spend time with You, listening to Your voice, every day.

Day 209

Redeemed

"I have swept away your offenses like a cloud, your sins like the morning mist. Return to me, for I have redeemed you."
Isaiah 44:22 NIV

You are redeemed. Like Adam and Eve's sin did, our sin cast us out of God's presence forever. We lived cursed and condemned. But when Jesus hung on the cross, He took that curse upon Himself (Galatians 3:13). His sacrificial death on our behalf purchased our freedom and granted us forgiveness (Colossians 1:14). We can return to God's presence! We no longer must be separated from Him.

Is shame forcing you away from God? Does guilt cause you to keep God at a distance? You are *redeemed*, girl! Your guilt and shame are gone. Your sins have been paid for. Return to the loving arms of your Father. He loves you. He forgives you. He wants you to come home to Him.

> Jesus, I am overwhelmed at the price You paid to redeem me. The depth of Your love for me is hard to grasp. Redeem my past mistakes, and use what brings me shame to bring You glory.

Day 210

A Willingness for God's Will

Then Jesus went away a second time and prayed, "My Father, if it is not possible for this painful thing to be taken from me, and if I must do it, I pray that what you want will be done."
Matthew 26:42 NCV

Life doesn't always turn out the way you'd hoped. Sometimes you face situations you'd rather completely skip. Jesus understands.

Instead of ignoring His feelings, Jesus honestly prayed. He asked His Father to change the situation and take it away from Him. When you pray, you can follow Jesus' example and honestly talk to God about your feelings.

After He shared how He felt, Jesus made an important decision: "If I must do it, I pray that what you want will be done." That attitude and decision are essential to a life of faith. Ask God for His will to be done, no matter what you might feel.

My Father, if I must do what I don't want to do, I pray that what You want will be done.

Day 211

Dealing with Guilt and Shame

I prayed, "My God, I am too ashamed and embarrassed to lift up my face to you, my God, because our sins are so many. They are higher than our heads. Our guilt even reaches up to the sky."

Ezra 9:6 NCV

No matter how good of a life you think you're living, when you realize how holy and perfect God is, your own imperfections are magnified. It can feel embarrassing to come to the Lord in prayer when you feel the shame or disgust of your sin.

In the Bible, Ezra and the Israelites dealt with guilt and shame. Their sins, too many to count, weighed heavily on their consciences. But Ezra came to the Lord in prayer anyway. He asked for forgiveness, and the Israelites turned away from their sins to pursue the Lord.

You can do the same! When you realize your sins, pray for forgiveness. Ask the Lord to help you turn around and stop sinning.

God, I am too ashamed and embarrassed because my sins are so many. Please forgive me! Please help me live a life that pleases You.

Day 212

Laying Down Our Life

We know what real love is from Christ's example in dying for us. And so we also ought to lay down our lives for our Christian brothers.

1 John 3:16 TLB

This is a call for us to be inconvenienced for the sake of others. To *lay down our lives*—while it can mean exactly what it says—also means to put others before you. It means being the hands and feet of Jesus to those who need help. It's bringing His hope to the hopeless. How can you do that in your community, in the classroom, in a church, at a job, or on the court? Ask God to show you, and then watch for opportunities to present themselves.

Maybe it's volunteering your time. Maybe it's befriending the outcast. Maybe it's donating to a shelter. Or it may be tangibly meeting the needs of those you know or love. Today, ask God to use you in extraordinary ways. By doing this, you're choosing to love just as the scriptures say. And it's a powerful expression of God's work in your heart.

Lord, use me to bless others. Amen.

Day 213

Yes, You Might Be Insulted

If you are insulted because you bear the name of Christ, you will be blessed, for the glorious Spirit of God rests upon you.

1 Peter 4:14 NLT

Choosing Jesus means you may be insulted if you're doing your best to follow Him and obey God's Word. What's cool and popular in the world is often so opposite of what God's Word says is good and right. And when you don't go along with what's cool and popular, there's a good chance someone will make fun of you. That's not easy to deal with, but you can handle it. You are strong and brave because of the power of Jesus in you. He promises to bless you, and His Holy Spirit never, ever leaves you.

Jesus, I'll keep on choosing You and following You and am happy to be called a Christian no matter what anyone else says about me. You make me strong and brave, and You fill my life with blessings. Amen.

Day 214

Wants and Needs

And my God will supply all your needs according to His riches in glory in Christ Jesus.
PHILIPPIANS 4:19 NASB

Have you ever wanted chocolate for breakfast? You may have felt like you *needed* that chocolate. But as delicious as it is, chocolate is usually more of a want than a need. This verse addresses the difference between those two.

God isn't some Santa-in-the-sky, fulfilling a never-ending wish list. He's way more concerned about your character than whether or not you have the most expensive designer shoes. But He will give you everything you need. So if you *need* a nice pair of shoes, He'll make sure you have them. He'll supply you with good friends, but you have to do the work to build the relationships. He'll provide you with opportunities to use your strengths for His glory, things that will help you feel fulfilled and satisfied with your life.

Trust Him for everything. He will supply all you need.

Father, right now I need ____. I trust You completely.

Day 215

Chosen

"I no longer call you slaves, because a master doesn't confide in his slaves. Now you are my friends, since I have told you everything the Father told me. You didn't choose me. I chose you."

John 15:15–16 NLT

You are chosen. God calls you His friend when you are obedient to Him (John 15:14). Jesus desires to confide in you and reveal to you what the Father reveals to Him. He has written your name on the palms of His hands as a sign that He will never forget you (Isaiah 49:15–16). Even if your father and mother abandon you, the Lord will gladly take you in (Psalm 27:10). He takes great delight in you and rejoices over you with singing (Zephaniah 3:17). The infinite, almighty Creator of the universe chose *you* to be His friend! The world may reject you, but you can overcome any rejection with the confidence of God's love and friendship.

Jesus, I'm so blown away that You would choose me to be Your friend. When I feel rejected and left out, help me remember how much I'm truly loved.

Day 216

Asking for Forgiveness

Lord, don't correct me when you are angry; don't punish me when you are very angry. Lord, have mercy on me because I am weak. Heal me, Lord, because my bones ache. I am very upset. Lord, how long will it be?

Psalm 6:1–3 NCV

Every single person sins. As much as you might try to intentionally live a perfect life, you'll make mistakes. You'll choose responses that aren't right. Your sin and wrong choices will separate you from God and His perfection.

Even if you feel pulled to make a wrong choice or if you know you've done something to upset the Lord, you can still come to Him. You don't have to hide away in shame. When you know you've done wrong, simply tell Him. Admit your mistake, ask for forgiveness, and be grateful for the Lord's mercy.

Lord, please forgive me! I've done wrong and I'm sorry. Please don't punish me. Instead, please have mercy on me!

Day 217

Help!

LORD, my Rock, I call out to you for help. Do not be deaf to me. If you are silent, I will be like those in the grave. Hear the sound of my prayer, when I cry out to you for help.

PSALM 28:1–2 NCV

Just like you'd ask for help whenever you feel stuck in a situation, call out to God for help too. Simply pray without speaking a word. Communicate with the Lord through your thoughts. And as your mind is racing and you know you need help or understanding or guidance, ask Him. Call out to Him for help, either by saying the words out loud or to yourself.

When you do call out to Him for help, you might feel like you're waiting endlessly for Him to respond. Know that He does hear you, and even if you don't see immediate results, He is answering your prayer in His own way.

Lord, my Rock, help! Please listen to my prayer. I need Your help!

Day 218

Actions and Words Align

Little children, let us stop just saying we love people;
let us really love them, and show it by our actions.

1 John 3:18 TLB

Actions always speak louder than words. Think about it. You can tell your little brother you love him, but will you show it when he frustrates you? Will you be kind to your beloved coach when she pulls you from the court? Will your friendship stay intact when your bestie makes a mistake that hurts you?

The truth is it's easy to tell someone you love them. Those words can flow freely and often. But when a relationship faces difficulties and discouragements, will you choose to let your actions convey the same love? Let's make sure how we act aligns with what we say. And when it's a struggle, let's ask God for help so we can be consistent for those we care about.

Lord, I confess the times my words and actions have not aligned. Help me love others consistently in what I say and in what I do so no doubts arise in their heart. Amen.

Day 219

With Jesus, You Are Always Stronger

The One Who lives in you is stronger than the one who is in the world.

1 JOHN 4:4 NLV

Our enemy, the devil, is stirring up all kinds of evil in this world. And you will be under attack from him and from the power of sin in all sorts of ways—through someone else's unkind words or actions, through stressful times for your family, through painful times of loss, through sickness, and so on. You can probably make a list right now, unfortunately. But no matter how strong the enemy and his evil seem, the devil is never stronger than the power of God in you through the Holy Spirit—all because you have chosen Jesus as your Savior.

Jesus, sometimes I forget the truth that You are always stronger than any evil attack against me, any hard thing I'm going through. Please remind me and fill me with Your strength and power through the Holy Spirit. Amen.

Day 220

In the Morning

For His anger is but for a moment, His favor is for a lifetime; weeping may last for the night, but a shout of joy comes in the morning.

PSALM 30:5 NASB

Have you ever gotten in trouble or had a really bad day? For that moment, everything felt wrong. You may have wondered if things would ever be right again. You may have even cried yourself to sleep, only to wake up feeling better about things. That's how it is with God, only on a much greater scale.

Circumstances are temporary. But God's love for you? It's permanent. It can never be changed or moved or minimized in any way. And His love means He wants you to know the joy only He gives. If you're miserable right now—if you cry yourself to sleep at night and fight tears even during the day—hang in there. You are one of His favorites, and He has good, happy, joyful things in store for you. . .sooner than you think.

Thank You for Your promise of joy. Please bring it soon.

Day 221

Never Alone

Where could I go to escape from your Spirit or from your sight? If I were to climb up to the highest heavens, you would be there. If I were to dig down to the world of the dead you would also be there. . . . Or suppose I said, "I'll hide in the dark until night comes to cover me over." But you see in the dark because daylight and dark are all the same to you.

Psalm 139:7–8, 11–12 CEV

You are never alone. God's presence is with you—all the time, everywhere. You may feel broken, abandoned, used, or unloved, but here's the truth: Nothing you've done or experienced will ever change God's love for you. His presence stays with you wherever you try to hide. Even if you're in a rebellious state, God doesn't abandon you but longs for your return (Luke 15:11–31). God may not be pleased with your behavior, but God's displeasure with disobedience is separate from His love for you. His love never wavers. His presence never disappears. His arms are always open.

Lord, You see me, and You never leave me, even when I run from You.

Day 222

Entertaining Angels

Do not neglect hospitality to strangers, for by this some have entertained angels without knowing it.
Hebrews 13:2 NASB

Imagine heaven and earth overlapping through your act of kindness. There's so much about the spiritual realm that remains a mystery to us, but throughout the Bible we're told about angels and how they take on many forms.

By showing hospitality to strangers, you might very well be serving angels. It's crazy to think about! Our hearts and motives are put to the test through angels in disguise because, in the words of former publisher Malcolm Forbes, "You can easily judge the character of others by how they treat those who can do nothing for them."

Dear God, I can't imagine coming face-to-face with an angel! Through my kindness, I want to be the kind of person who entertains angels without realizing it.

Day 223

Believe and Love

And this is what God says we must do: Believe on the name of his Son Jesus Christ, and love one another.
1 John 3:23 TLB

What are the ways you show love and kindness toward others? Maybe you pay attention in class when your teacher is speaking. Maybe you are verbally affirming to the new youth leader at church. Maybe you spend quality time with your grandparents regularly. Maybe you cook a meal or clean around the house without being asked. Or maybe you find intentional ways to show appreciation to those around you.

These acts of kindness come from a heart invested in a relationship with the Lord. It's from Him that we're able to love others selflessly. He gives us the desire to choose compassionate ways to bless those we care for. And the time we spend deepening our faith creates a softening inside, leading us toward feelings of love.

Lord, I do believe in You, and I know it's why I am able to love others with fervor. Let it always be so. Amen.

Day 224

Humble Servant Leader

After Jesus had washed his disciples' feet. . .he said: Do you understand what I have done? You call me your teacher and Lord, and you should, because that is who I am. And if your Lord and teacher has washed your feet, you should do the same for each other. I have set the example, and you should do for each other exactly what I have done for you. I tell you for certain that servants are not greater than their master, and messengers are not greater than the one who sent them. You know these things, and God will bless you, if you do them.

John 13:12–17 CEV

Jesus is King of kings and Lord of lords. Everyone on earth will bow down to Him one day. At the same time, He is truly a humble servant leader. He showed an example of that when He washed His disciples' feet. And He taught that they should do the same and that they would be blessed for being humble servants of each other. That message was not just for the disciples; it's for us too.

Jesus, thank You for showing us how to be humble and have compassion, how to serve and love others. I want to be like You and treat others like You do. Amen.

Day 225

Steadfast

The steadfast of mind You will keep in perfect peace, because he trusts in You.

Isaiah 26:3 NASB

The word *steadfast* is a fancy, old-fashioned word with a simple meaning. To be steadfast means to be reliable, dependable, loyal, and steady. Many people are the opposite of steadfast when it comes to faith in God. They call out to Him when they're desperate but ignore Him when things are good. Just like you don't feel great when a "friend" only calls when they need something, God reacts the same way.

But those who are steadfast, who praise Him in the good times and trust Him when it's hard, those are the people God counts as His true friends. And those are the people He rewards with a beautiful inner peace that's hard for others to understand.

More than anything, I want to be Your steadfast friend, Lord. I know every good thing is from You, and I'm so grateful for Your love and generosity. I know You alone can guide me through the hard times, and I'll trust You no matter what.

Day 226

Securely Held

I am God now and forever. No one can snatch you from me or stand in my way.

ISAIAH 43:13 CEV

You are securely held. God is your ultimate bodyguard. No power even remotely matches His. He fights for you against Satan's lies and schemes. His love chases you when you run away from Him. He lights up the shadows when you're surrounded by darkness. His power kicks down all the barriers standing in the way of where He wants you to go. He protects you and guards your heart and mind with peace when you're flooded with fear.

Do you see the fierce way He loves and protects you? Do you see the awesomeness of His incomparable power? Do you see the security and safety you have in His care? Rest in confidence and peace that you have someone in your corner who is always fighting for you, shielding you, and watching over you. God's got you, and He'll never let go!

God, Your love for me is overwhelming. Thank You for claiming me, fiercely guarding me, and never letting me go!

Day 227

Everyday Blessings

Say to him, "Save us, God our Savior, and bring us back and save us from other nations. Then we will thank you and will gladly praise you." Praise the Lord*, the God of Israel. He always was and always will be. All the people said "Amen" and praised the* Lord*.*

1 Chronicles 16:35–36 NCV

The Israelites, God's chosen people, were able to think back on all the ways the Lord rescued them throughout their history. When they were conquered by other nations, over and over the Lord saved them and brought them back to their land. Because of His faithful rescue, time and time again, they thanked and praised Him.

Like the Israelites, when you spy God at work in your life, thank Him! Praise Him for the ways He works the miraculous, whether you notice big gifts from Him or tiny ones. Look for Him at work in your day, and every day you'll find evidence of the way He loves and saves you.

God my Savior, I praise You! Thank You for the way You rescue me. You always were and always will be. I gladly praise You.

Day 228

Owing Others Love

Owe nothing to anyone—except for your obligation to love one another. If you love your neighbor, you will fulfill the requirements of God's law.
Romans 13:8 NLT

Consider that the Lord wants you to owe nothing but love to others. It's not a joy-draining demand but a life-giving command that brings blessings to all involved. Even more, it's not a one-and-done concept. Instead, God wants us to see it as an ongoing effort. It should be our pleasure and passion to love others well.

Is it always easy to do? No, ma'am. Often, it takes grit and grace we can only get from the Lord. Does it come easily? Sometimes, yes! But other times loving others is a choice. In those moments, we must decide to show kindness and compassion to the unlovable with a pure heart. And with God's strength, we can do it.

Lord, shift my heart and mind to understand the value in loving others consistently. It's not only a command but also a privilege. And I will choose every day to love in Your strength. Amen.

Day 229

The Good News

And then he told them, "Go into all the world and preach the Good News to everyone."
MARK 16:15 NLT

Every human being is born into this world affected by sin. The good news of the gospel, however, is that Jesus took care of the penalty for sin when He died on the cross. If you've put your trust in Jesus as your Savior, then you have received healing and are no longer under the curse of sin!

The kindest thing you can do for a person is tell them about this gift. Not everyone will want it, but in sharing that it exists, people who've been searching for hope will find life!

Dear God, I want people to know what Jesus did on the cross for them! Please give me boldness to speak the truth about this good news to everyone.

Day 230

Our Perfect Home Forever

"Do not let your hearts be troubled. You believe in God; believe also in me. My Father's house has many rooms; if that were not so, would I have told you that I am going there to prepare a place for you? And if I go and prepare a place for you, I will come back and take you to be with me that you also may be where I am. You know the way to the place where I am going."

John 14:1–4 NIV

Our perfect forever home is waiting for us in heaven—in God's house! Jesus talked about its many rooms. Those rooms will be far cooler than anything we can imagine! We can talk to Jesus anytime and tell Him what we hope heaven will be like, and then we can tell Him that we simply trust it will be the very best because we will live with Him there.

Jesus, I believe that heaven will be awesome! I'm so thankful You have saved me from my sin so that I get to spend forever at home with You! Amen.

Day 231

Self-Talk

Why are you in despair, my soul? And why are you restless within me? Wait for God, for I will again praise Him for the help of His presence, my God.
PSALM 42:5 NASB

Do you talk to yourself? We all do. If we say negative things inside our heads, we have a poor outlook on life. But if we say encouraging things, our attitude improves.

In this psalm, David gives himself a pep talk. He says, "Why are you sad? You know God is working. You know He has good things in store. One day soon, you'll praise Him for all the great things He's done. Just wait!"

Next time you feel sad, angry, or anxious, give yourself a pep talk. Remind yourself to wait on God, because He's working on your behalf. Remember His presence in your life and that you're never alone. And tell yourself that soon you'll be praising Him for something even better than you can imagine.

I know You're working things out for my good, Father. Help me adjust my self-talk to reflect Your love for me.

Day 232

Intrinsic Value

So God created human beings in his own image. In the image of God he created them; male and female he created them.
GENESIS 1:27 NLT

You have value. But that value isn't because of how you look or because you belong to the right teams or clubs or because you're smart. Strip away all your talents and abilities, and you still have value. Why? Because you're made in the image of God. Of everything God created, He only stamped His divine image on humans. That means He's placed something intrinsic in you that reflects who He is.

Imagine a diamond ring falls to the ground and gets trampled on. Dirty and dented, does it still have the same value? Of course! The world tries to make you feel like you don't have value unless you dress, behave, and believe a certain way. People will mistreat you, use you, and bully you. But no matter how dirty and dented you may feel, your value has never changed. How does that assurance alter how you see yourself?

> God, so often I feel like my value is in my looks or abilities. But my value comes from You and can't be lost or changed.

Day 233

Faith and Trust

But let him ask in faith, with no doubting, for the one who doubts is like a wave of the sea that is driven and tossed by the wind.
JAMES 1:6 ESV

James talks a lot about faith and what that looks like. In chapter 2, he says God called Abraham His friend because of his faith. Even when God told Abraham to leave his home and go but didn't tell him where he was going, Abraham obeyed. He trusted God completely.

If we want God to call us His friends, we must not doubt His love for us. No matter what happens, He wants us to believe that He's in control and that the outcome will be good. We don't have to like everything that happens, but we can have faith that God knows what He's doing. Even when we don't understand, we can trust His heart for us. When we ask God for answers or changes or miracles, trust Him. Leave it with Him. He will take care of you.

I trust You, Lord. Help me trust You more.

Day 234

Holy, Holy, Holy

Each of the four living creatures had six wings and was covered with eyes all around, even under its wings. Day and night they never stop saying: "'Holy, holy, holy is the Lord God Almighty,' who was, and is, and is to come."

Revelation 4:8 niv

Heaven contains sights and sounds and experiences we can never fully imagine in this earthly life. When writers of the Bible try to describe certain scenes, it's hard to comprehend. Living creatures with six wings and a bunch of eyes? It sounds like something that belongs in a science fiction movie.

Besides the unusual description of the creatures, notice what they spend all their time saying: "'Holy, holy, holy is the Lord God Almighty,' who was, and is, and is to come."

Just like that's being proclaimed in heaven, you also can declare it right now in your prayers. When you pray to God, remember that He is holy, meaning blameless, pure, and set apart. Remember He's always been holy. He is holy right at this moment. And He is holy for all of eternity to come.

Holy, holy, holy are You, Lord God Almighty!

Day 235

The Law of Love

Love does no wrong to anyone. That's why it fully satisfies all of God's requirements. It is the only law you need.
ROMANS 13:10 TLB

The Word of God says the only law we need is the law to love. Think about that for a moment, considering how that choice impacts every relationship in your life.

When you choose to love your parents, you obey their rules without complaining. When you choose to love your friends, you celebrate their accomplishments rather than be jealous of them. By choosing to love your teammates and coaches, time off the court and on the bench doesn't upset you. Loving others means not participating in gossip. It means being generous with your time. It's being cooperative rather than complaining. And it informs how you respond, making sure you're showing compassion and care in the right moments.

Be the kind of young woman who does no wrong to anyone. This isn't a call to be perfect but to be purposeful in how you treat others.

Lord, help me choose to love others well. Give me the ability to follow this powerful law, even when it feels impossible to do so. Amen.

Day 236

Take a Rest

By the seventh day God had finished the work he had been doing; so on the seventh day he rested from all his work. Then God blessed the seventh day and made it holy, because on it he rested from all the work of creating that he had done.

Genesis 2:2–3 niv

If we're going to be effective workers for the kingdom, we must learn to rest. God set an example for us by resting after six days of creating. As beings created in His image, we're meant to take breaks from our work.

Taking a set time away from your daily routine will revive your spirit and reset your focus. Consider taking a day—or a few hours if a full day is impossible—to take a break from "life." This might require a little bit of advanced planning if you need to get ahead with homework or do some chores, but when you commit to resting your body and mind every now and then, you'll be better equipped to make kind choices.

Dear Lord, I know rest is important.
Give me opportunities to rest and restore my soul!

Day 237

Super Generous Forgiveness

Peter came to Jesus and asked, "Lord, how many times shall I forgive my brother or sister who sins against me? Up to seven times?" Jesus answered, "I tell you, not seven times, but seventy-seven times."

MATTHEW 18:21–22 NIV

Jesus is not stingy or cheap with forgiveness. He's super generous about it, and He taught us to be too. When His disciple Peter asked how many times he should forgive someone sinning against him, Jesus answered that whatever amount we first think is right, we should go way above and beyond that amount—because Jesus goes way above and beyond at loving and forgiving us! That's an incredible blessing, and we should want to share that blessing.

Jesus, please help me to do my best at forgiving others in over-the-top, above-and-beyond kinds of ways like You forgive me. Amen.

Day 238

What Faith Does

"Truly, I say to you, if you have faith and do not doubt, you will not only do what has been done to the fig tree, but even if you say to this mountain, 'Be taken up and thrown into the sea,' it will happen."

MATTHEW 21:21 ESV

In the verses before this, Jesus was hungry. He saw a fig tree and decided to get a snack, but there were no figs. Jesus cursed the tree. "May you never bear fruit again!" Immediately, the tree withered. His disciples were amazed and asked how He caused it to wither so quickly. His answer was the verse above.

We may not need to move mountains. But we may need to get into a certain school. We may need help as we study for a test. We may need the right words to say when there are no words to express our feelings. And so much more! Trust Him for the miracles you need in your life. Don't doubt. He will deliver.

I want this kind of faith, Lord. Teach me to trust You.

Day 239

Planned for a Purpose

You are the one who put me together inside my mother's body,
and I praise you because of the wonderful way you created
me. . . . Nothing about me is hidden from you! I was secretly
woven together out of human sight, but with your own eyes
you saw my body being formed. Even before I was born,
you had written in your book everything about me.

Psalm 139:13–16 CEV

You are created for a purpose. Some of us can say we were born "on accident"—our parents weren't trying to get pregnant. But no one can say God created us "on accident." Your existence was purposeful and planned by our amazing Creator. He lovingly formed you in your mother's womb because He knew this world needed *you*.

You play a specific role that can only be filled by you. You have a purpose. Whether your parents "planned" you or not, you were most definitely planned and wanted by the Father!

Lord, I am no accident to You. I have value and purpose in Your eyes. Please guide me and show me the plans and purposes You intend for me.

Day 240

Every Good Thing

Protect me, God, because I trust in you. I said to the Lord, "You are my Lord. Every good thing I have comes from you."

Psalm 16:1–2 NCV

How would your life be different if you realized that every good thing you have comes from God?

Instead of thinking you deserve blessings or work hard enough to make good things happen, you'll find that when you begin to realize that all the good that happens to you comes from the Lord.

God will protect you. Not only is He a protective Father, but He also is trustworthy. He knows when you trust Him, and He loves to lavish you with good gifts. Take just a moment to think about every good thing in your life. You might think of things that happened today or things that happened years ago. Think about the good and thank God for each of these good, good gifts.

Lord, I do trust You. You are my Lord! Thank You so much for every good thing I have. They are good, good gifts from You.

Day 241

A Beautiful By-Product

We know how much God loves us because we have felt his love and because we believe him when he tells us that he loves us dearly. God is love, and anyone who lives in love is living with God and God is living in him.

1 John 4:16 TLB

Simply put, love is a beautiful by-product of being a true believer of Jesus. We read about God's deep love for us in the Bible. We feel His love in our life as we supernaturally receive what we need to navigate each situation. And God shows us His love as we experience His goodness in each day, regardless of our circumstances. Because He is love, it's an unavoidable blessing and gift. That means we can access it whenever we need it.

Ask God to help you choose to love others in meaningful ways. Give them your time. Speak kind words. Be willing to help. Listen when they need it. Pray when asked. Show compassion and give care without hesitation.

Lord, thank You for being love, because it allows me to show it to others. You think of everything. Amen.

Day 242

Known by Our Love

"By this all people will know that you are my disciples, if you have love for one another."
JOHN 13:35 ESV

If you follow Jesus, then you're an ambassador for God's kingdom. You represent Christ here on earth. When people look at you, they get a glimpse of Jesus.

As a Christ follower, your life will look different. One of the biggest things people notice is how Christians treat other people. Complaining, gossiping, and holding grudges are typical behaviors of the world. Instead, love, serve, and speak well of all people, but especially your brothers and sisters in Christ. Build them up and encourage them. By this the world will look and say, "Oh, that's unique!"

Dear God, help me love my brothers and sisters in Christ in such a way that the world knows my devotion to You!

Day 243

Jesus and Lazarus

They took away the stone. Then Jesus looked up and said, "Father, I thank you that you have heard me. I knew that you always hear me, but I said this for the benefit of the people standing here, that they may believe that you sent me." When he had said this, Jesus called in a loud voice, "Lazarus, come out!" The dead man came out, his hands and feet wrapped with strips of linen, and a cloth around his face. Jesus said to them, "Take off the grave clothes and let him go."

JOHN 11:41–44 NIV

Jesus completely amazed the people when he healed his friend Lazarus, who had been dead for four days. But Jesus did this to help people believe in Him as God and choose Him as Savior and receive forgiveness of sins and eternal life beyond this world. He had said this to Martha just before He called her brother Lazarus out of the tomb: "I am the resurrection and the life. The one who believes in me will live, even though they die; and whoever lives by believing in me will never die. Do you believe this?" (John 11:25–26 NIV).

Jesus, yes, I believe You are the resurrection and the life! Amen.

Day 244

Whatever You Ask

And whatever we ask we receive from him, because we keep his commandments and do what pleases him.

1 John 3:22 ESV

At first glance, this verse makes God seem like a jolly Santa Claus granting our never-ending wish lists. But this promise comes with a condition. You can't take the first part of the verse without the second part. If "we keep his commandments and do what pleases Him," He will grant whatever we ask.

When we obey Him and seek to please Him, our desires begin to line up with His goals for us. Our obedience begins a slow transformation into the people He wants us to be. As our hearts change to reflect His character, our requests change. It doesn't happen overnight. It's a lifelong process.

The good news is, God is pleased with our sincere efforts to please Him—no matter how imperfect they may be. And when He's pleased with our hearts, He likes to bless us.

I know I can ask You anything, Father.
Transform my heart so my desires are the same as Yours.

Day 245

Place to Belong

Through Christ, God has given us the privilege and authority as apostles to tell Gentiles everywhere what God has done for them, so that they will believe and obey him, bringing glory to his name. And you are included among those Gentiles who have been called to belong to Jesus Christ.

Romans 1:5–6 NLT

You belong to Jesus. The question of where we belong often plagues us. You may feel like you don't really belong at school. You have friends, but you don't have a close circle of friends. You're always on the fringe, never fully part of a group. Not feeling accepted can really feed our insecurity and shake our confidence. When you find yourself searching for a place to belong, repeat this truth to yourself: "I belong to Jesus."

Jesus accepts you. He claims you as His own. He warmly welcomes you into His circle of friends. Spend time with Him each day and let His love wrap around you like a cozy blanket, giving you the security and confidence you need.

> Jesus, help me always remember I belong to You. Help me also find a healthy place to belong here.

Day 246

More About Mountains

"Truly, I say to you, whoever says to this mountain, 'Be taken up and thrown into the sea,' and does not doubt in his heart, but believes that what he says will come to pass, it will be done for him."

MARK 11:23 ESV

A few pages back, we read Matthew 21:21. Here, we read about that mountain again! When we talk to God about something but then do whatever we want, that's not strong faith. When we ask Him to take care of a problem then manipulate things to work out how we want, that's trusting ourselves, not God.

What mountains do you need to overcome? Talk to God. Tell Him how you'd like things to work out but leave it all in His hands. Trust Him to do what's best, even if it doesn't look exactly like you pictured. God loves that kind of faith, and He will move heaven and earth—or a mountain—for the one who trusts Him completely.

Father, You know the mountains I face. You're the only one who can move them. I trust You completely.

Day 247

The Agony of Enemies

LORD, I have many enemies! Many people have turned against me. Many are saying about me, "God won't rescue him." But, LORD, you are my shield, my wonderful God who gives me courage.

PSALM 3:1–3 NCV

It's no fun to know you have enemies, whether they're frenemies you pretend to get along with or outright enemies who make your life miserable. When people turn against you, it leaves you feeling awful.

If and when you're dealing with frustration, hurt, or anger that comes along with enemies, don't try to figure things out on your own. As tempting as it is to dwell on your negative thoughts and feelings, turn things over to the Lord. Ask Him for help, along with some comfort and strength. Pray that He will protect you and give you courage to deal with the situation. Ask Him to rescue you. Trust that He will work all things out for good.

Lord, You are my shield. Please protect me as I deal with all the hurt that comes with having enemies. Please rescue me from this situation! Protect me and give me courage.

Day 248

Don't Pretend to Love

Don't just pretend that you love others: really love them. Hate what is wrong. Stand on the side of the good.
ROMANS 12:9 TLB

Chances are you know what it feels like when others pretend to care about you. You've probably experienced fake love from people you thought were friends, only to later discover how they really felt. And when you did, it just felt lousy.

God wants us to choose to really, truly love others instead. What might that look like in your life? Remember that He's looking for authenticity not driven by dishonest and selfish motives. He wants us to steer clear of what is wrong and align ourselves with what is good. We're to love those around us in meaningful ways that bless them and glorify God. And at every opportunity, we're to exercise compassion and kindness toward others. How are you doing with that?

Lord, help me show faithful love. Help me be genuine. Dependable. And whenever I come to a crossroads of options, may I choose to stand on the side of good and love others well. Amen.

Day 249

Take Your Worries to Jesus

Then Jesus said, "Come to me, all of you who are weary and carry heavy burdens, and I will give you rest."
MATTHEW 11:28 NLT

Let's face it, sometimes life gets incredibly hard. If you're overwhelmed by the heaviness of the world, then run, limp, or crawl as fast as you can into the arms of Jesus!

True rest is found in the arms of the Savior, who loves you and holds you close during the worst moments of your life. He'll restore your confidence and remind you of your worth.

When you feel like you can't go on, the author and perfecter of your faith draws you close to Him, reminding you that you're loved, protected, and cherished.

Dear heavenly Father, sometimes life gets really discouraging and it's hard to find any hope. I want You to take my hurts and fears and replace them with purpose and peace.

Day 250

Before You Ask

[Jesus said:] "Your Father knows what you need before you ask him."
MATTHEW 6:8 ESV

If Jesus taught that your heavenly Father knows what you need before you even ask Him, you might say, "Why should I pray at all? God already knows!" And the answer is "Because God loves you that much, that's why!" He wants a close relationship with you that much. He wants to hear from you even though He already knows everything about you and everything you need!

Really think about that for a minute—the God of the whole universe wants to be in close relationship with you. That's incredible! The fact that He already knows everything about you plus everything about *everything* is a reason to want to talk to Him all the more, never a reason to think you don't need to bother.

Jesus, thank You for teaching me about God's great love for me. Amen.

Day 251

Choosing Friends

One who walks with wise people will be wise,
but a companion of fools will suffer harm.
PROVERBS 13:20 NASB

The world wants us to embrace diversity and all kinds of differences. That's good, because God loves diversity! He created us all different and unique. But when it comes to choosing friends, we tend to rise or sink to the level of the people around us.

While we should love everyone and treat all people with respect and kindness, we must be careful about who we choose as close friends. Remember, Christ loved everyone but kept only a small group of men in His inner circle. To follow Christ's example, we need to love everyone but share our secrets and spend lots of time only with people we trust, who share our values, and who want to please God.

Lord, I need good friends, but they can be hard to find. Please lead me to people who will be good, wise friends. Help me be that kind of friend to others.

Day 252

God's Masterpiece

For we are God's masterpiece.
Ephesians 2:10 NLT

You are God's masterpiece. Merriam-Webster defines *masterpiece* as "a work done with extraordinary skill" and "a supreme intellectual or artistic achievement." God created you with extraordinary skill, carefully choosing just the right shade of your skin, eyes, and hair. No one on earth looks exactly the same. (Even twins are slightly different!)

You are God's masterpiece because there is no one else like you—and there never will be. Don't throw shade on God's supreme artistic achievement by hating certain parts of your body. "My thighs are so big." "I hate my hair." "My nose is so embarrassing!" God lovingly crafted each part of you. Don't insult Him by thinking ugly thoughts about yourself—or others. The enemy wants to destroy your beauty by making you discontented and by making you believe lies about how you look. Stand confident in your identity as God's masterpiece. You are beautiful!

Wow, God, it's mind-blowing to consider the billions and billions of masterpieces You've made! And I'm one of them. Help me see myself through Your eyes and appreciate Your skill instead of hating certain parts of my body.

Day 253

Jealousy

For where jealousy and selfish ambition exist,
there is disorder and every evil thing.
JAMES 3:16 NASB

If someone else has something we want, it's hard not to envy that. But jealousy can destroy our happiness. If we want God's best for us, we must set aside our ideas about what we want and embrace what God wants for us. And we must put others first and be happy for their blessings instead of mad that we didn't get the same thing.

When we get caught up in jealousy, we become mean, bitter, and angry. Next time you feel a twinge of envy because someone else has something you want, ask God to change your heart. Try to be happy for that person, then spend some time thanking Him for all the unique ways He's blessed you.

Sometimes jealous feelings show up in my heart so quickly, I didn't see them coming. Help me recognize jealousy and set it aside just as quickly. Teach me to be happy for others. Thank You for all You've given me.

Day 254

Why?

Moses returned to the Lord *and said, "Why, Lord, why have you brought trouble on this people? Is this why you sent me? Ever since I went to Pharaoh to speak in your name, he has brought trouble on this people, and you have not rescued your people at all."*

Exodus 5:22–23 NIV

Moses knew the Lord set him apart to help lead the Israelites out of Egypt. Even if it was time for the Israelites to be set free from their bondage, the Egyptians didn't welcome this news. In fact, Pharaoh refused to set the Israelites free, and he increased their workload. Moses' response to these circumstances was prayer. When he didn't understand what was going on, he shared all the details and asked God for clarity.

Like Moses' life, things may not seem to be working out the way you'd hoped. Instead of focusing on everything that's gone wrong, though, pray. Describe your situation to the Lord, ask Him for help, and then wait to watch Him work.

Lord, why have You let bad things happen? I wasn't prepared for the disappointment and struggle that I'm facing. Please work in this situation.

Day 255

Nothing Is Too Hard

"I prayed to the LORD, Oh, Lord GOD, you made the skies and the earth with your very great power. There is nothing too hard for you to do."

JEREMIAH 32:16–17 NCV

How easy is it to focus on difficulties and what seems to be impossible? While you can get trapped in a thought pattern of focusing on the negative, it's important to learn from Jeremiah's prayer. There is nothing too hard for God to do. Nothing!

When you consider all the Lord has made, from the skies to the earth to all living creatures, He is the God who makes the impossible possible. This great God is worthy of your worship!

As you find yourself facing what seems to be an impossible situation, remind yourself that nothing is too hard for God to do. Then praise and pray to the God of the impossible.

Lord God, nothing is too hard for You to do! I praise You for Your mighty power and the way You do the impossible.

Day 256

Satisfied with God's Ways

Don't copy the behavior and customs of this world, but be a new and different person with a fresh newness in all you do and think. Then you will learn from your own experience how his ways will really satisfy you.

ROMANS 12:2 TLB

Be a breath of fresh air to those around you. Rather than fall in line with what the world says is right or wrong, let God transform your heart to be a new creation who follows His way. Be a young woman who stands up for truth and advocates for others. Speak with kindness, but don't be a doormat. Treat everyone with respect. Be willing to listen first before you feel the need to speak. And remain resolved to stand firm in God's commands for your life without caving to peer pressure. This is choosing love—love for the Lord, love for yourself, and love for others.

While some may tell you differently, God's ways are satisfying. Live them out and see for yourself.

Lord, help me find a fresh newness by following Your will and ways. Let my heart be satisfied by You alone. Amen.

Day 257

Childlike Faith

[Jesus] said to them, "Let the children come to me. Don't stop them! For the Kingdom of God belongs to those who are like these children. I tell you the truth, anyone who doesn't receive the Kingdom of God like a child will never enter it."

MARK 10:14–15 NLT

As you look to the future, what are the things you're looking forward to about not being a teen anymore? What are the things you will miss? It's fun to hold on to childish youth in some ways, although it's good (and necessary) to grow and mature. It's great, then, that Jesus tells us we should always be childlike in the way we have a relationship with Him. When we're young, we're pretty carefree, eager, and enthusiastic. We have great love for and faith in our parents or caretakers. And in that same kind of way, Jesus wants us to remain like children forever—trusting in Him completely to provide for every need and eagerly enjoying His great love for us.

Jesus, even as I'm maturing, help me to always have childlike, enthusiastic love, joy, and faith in You. Amen.

Day 258

Holy and Perfect

Even before he made the world, God loved us and chose us in Christ to be holy and without fault in his eyes.
EPHESIANS 1:4 NLT

You are without fault in God's eyes. God is all-knowing. He knew before He created the world how this human project was gonna go down—that we'd mess it up and He would have to send Jesus to fix it. And He loved us so much—He wanted a relationship with us so badly—He chose to create the world anyway.

When we repent and accept Jesus' sacrifice on the cross on our behalf, God gives us a new identity. We're no longer guilty sinners deserving of punishment. In Christ, we are holy and without fault in His eyes! So that shame you feel? He doesn't see it! The guilt you carry? It's gone! It's *gone*. You are holy, blameless, forgiven, *free*. Stand tall, girl! Shed that shame and guilt that weighs you down and walk confidently in your identity as a girl clean and holy!

God, I look in the mirror every day and find so much fault with myself. But You don't! You see me as perfect and holy.

Day 259

The Company You Keep

Do not be deceived: "Bad company corrupts good morals."

1 Corinthians 15:33 NASB

Sometimes we try to be someone's friend in hopes of helping them be better. But it's a lot easier to pull someone down than to pull them up. As an example, stand on a chair and try to pull someone of equal size up to you while they try to pull you down. The person on the floor will almost always win.

We should always show love, kindness, and respect to others—even if we don't agree with their choices. But don't become close friends with someone whose values and morals don't line up with God's Word. Live for Him, and others will often be drawn to His presence in you. Your godly example will cause others to seek Christ for themselves. Guard your heart and trust the Holy Spirit to make changes in their lives.

Give me wisdom about who to hang around with, Lord. I want all my choices to please You.

Day 260

Confess It

I acknowledged my sin to You, and I did not hide my guilt; I said, "I will confess my wrongdoings to the LORD*"; and You forgave the guilt of my sin.*

PSALM 32:5 NASB

Admitting that you're wrong takes a lot of courage. It's humbling to acknowledge that you've made a mistake, whether intentionally or unintentionally. It's embarrassing to own up to your sin.

As much as King David was a man after God's heart, he also sinned. He discovered that when he tried to hide his sin, it only made him feel terrible. Confessing brought freedom.

When you do sin and confess it to the Lord, you'll find freedom. When you stop hiding your guilt and own up to what you've done wrong, He'll forgive you. Come to the Lord with your honest prayers and confession and experience His forgiveness and love.

Lord, I have sinned against You. I'm sorry! I don't want to hide my guilt and wrongdoing anymore. Please forgive me.

Day 261

Working Together as One

Just as there are many parts to our bodies, so it is with Christ's body. We are all parts of it, and it takes every one of us to make it complete, for we each have different work to do. So we belong to each other, and each needs all the others.

Romans 12:4–5 TLB

The truth is we need one another. God made us to be in community with a variety of other believers because we fit together to further His kingdom. An assortment of family and friends as well as a mixture of other people are important parts of your life and work together as one. Each brings different talents and skills that support the bigger picture of faith. And together, we are a force for goodness.

This is why we choose to love others. We need to be together in Christ! We can't stay in self-protection mode because we've been hurt by community in the past. It leaves a noticeable gap. So choose to embrace others and the collective God has designed for you to thrive in.

Lord, thank You for the gift of my community. Every day, let me choose it. Amen.

Day 262

Endless Distractions

Make the most of every opportunity in these evil days.
EPHESIANS 5:16 NLT

Have you ever opened up social media and thought, *I'll just watch one video*, or *I'll scroll real quick and then get going*, and then, before you knew it, two hours had passed?

We live in an era of endless distractions. Hundreds of apps, TV networks, and companies compete for our time, attention, and clicks. Many of these things are okay in moderation, but often they consume so much of our time that we miss out on opportunities to serve, connect, and enjoy the world around us.

Be aware of your screen time. You only get one shot at today. Will you spend it looking at a device, or will you spend it looking for opportunities to be a different kind of light in a world lit by screens?

Dear Jesus, I confess that I don't always manage my time in a way that honors You. Help me use technology wisely so that I don't miss opportunities for kindness.

Day 263

Plans and Steps

We can make our plans, but the LORD determines our steps.
PROVERBS 16:9 NLT

It's good to make goals and go after them, but as we do so, we must ask Jesus what His will is and be willing to change our plans if He directs us to. He will determine each of our steps—and even if it's hard sometimes, we need to willingly accept that. Sometimes His steps for us will match exactly what we hoped for, and sometimes He might want to teach us something totally different from what we wanted. But when we humbly follow Jesus anywhere He says to go, He is going to lead us along the very best paths and plans for our lives.

Jesus, please change my plans as You see fit. Help me to humbly trust and follow You because I love You and I know You love me. Amen.

Day 264

Complete Victory

No, in all these things we have complete victory through him who loved us!
ROMANS 8:37 GNT

You have complete victory through Jesus! Wow, what a powerful promise! What sins do you feel trapped under, like you can never get free? "I'll never be able to stop. . ." Cutting? Having sex? Starving yourself to stay skinny? Pleasing people for approval? Whatever your struggle, you can have complete victory through Jesus!

"I've tried to stop!" you say. "My weakness keeps pulling me back. This is just who I am." BIG FAT LIE!!! Sure, the battle for freedom includes setbacks, but a failure does not define who you are. You are a victor! Get up and battle again until you gain complete freedom. Gather a group of trusted friends who know your struggle and can support you. You may need counseling to identify root issues that cause your behavior.

No sin has greater power than Jesus, so don't give sin ultimate power in your life. You're not a *victim of*. Confidence chooses to say, "I'm a *victor over*!" In Christ you have *complete victory*!

Jesus, I claim victory over. . .

Day 265

About Revenge

Never repay evil for evil to anyone.
Respect what is right in the sight of all people.
ROMANS 12:17 NASB

Our human nature says that if someone hurts you, hurt them back. The world tells us to get revenge. But God's ways aren't the same as our ways, and His ways are always better. He says that if someone hurts you, respect them. Pray for them. Show them what God's love looks like.

That doesn't mean you have to put yourself in situations where you know you'll get hurt. God wants you to use wisdom and steer clear of people who mean you harm. But when hurtful things happen, let God be your defender. Let Him handle the justice part of it. Your job is to love God and love others, and He will take care of the rest.

When others hurt me, I want to hurt them back. I want them to pay for the way they've treated me. Help me set aside my pride, treat everyone with love, and trust You with the outcome, Lord.

Day 266

A Friendship with God

The LORD spoke to Moses face to face as a man speaks with his friend. . . . Moses said to the LORD, . . . "You have said to me, 'I know you very well, and I am pleased with you.' If I have truly pleased you, show me your plans so that I may know you and continue to please you."

EXODUS 33:11–13 NCV

From his birth to his death, Moses led an extraordinary life. One amazing fact is that the Lord spoke to Moses face-to-face, just like friends. Part of their friendship involved absolute honesty. Moses shared exactly what he felt and thought with the Lord. He didn't sugarcoat awkward situations or challenges he faced.

Like Moses, you can come to the Lord just like you would come to your friend. Tell Him everything that's on your mind. Your prayers can include all your thoughts and feelings, your happy moments and your fears. Be honest with the Lord and watch how your relationship with Him will grow.

Lord, I want to be Your friend! I want to be honest with You.

Day 267

With Brotherly Affection

Love each other with brotherly affection
and take delight in honoring each other.
Romans 12:10 TLB

When scripture tells us to love with brotherly affection, it means with deep warmth. This is a notable kindness and sympathy we extend. There's intentional care and compassion in our actions. Our words are affirming in meaningful ways, bringing hope and encouragement when times are trying. And it's often how we feel about our family and close friends.

Chances are, we'd agree there are times this is simpler to walk out than others. Some people are just easier to love. Regardless, God's Word is clear that we're to choose to love other believers even when it's challenging. Even more, we are to delight in it rather than doing so begrudgingly. Ask God to soften your heart so brotherly affection comes quickly and without stress. And then watch as He blesses your obedience and boosts their sense of significance.

Lord, sometimes loving others is the hardest choice to make. Would You help me do so through Your strength, allowing me to follow this command with purpose? Amen.

Day 268

God Redeems Evil

"Don't you see, you planned evil against me but God used those same plans for my good, as you see all around you right now—life for many people."
GENESIS 50:20 MSG

At the end of Genesis, we're told the story of Joseph. Joseph was betrayed by his brothers, sold into slavery, falsely accused of a crime, and then thrown into prison. He had every reason to be angry and bitter. Yet the Bible tells us he forgave those who hurt him.

Joseph knew God's plan for good overruled his brothers' plan for evil. Joseph ended up in a position of power in Egypt, and his wisdom helped save countless people from starvation during a famine. Joseph realized God used every injustice for His sovereign and good purposes.

There's so much evil in the world, Lord God. When things seem hopeless, help me remember that You're working everything for good.

Day 269

Detailed Love

[Jesus said:] "Are not two small birds sold for a very small piece of money? And yet not one of the birds falls to the earth without your Father knowing it. God knows how many hairs you have on your head. So do not be afraid. You are more important than many small birds."

MATTHEW 10:29–31 NLV

Jesus taught that there is no one who knows and loves you like your heavenly Father does. Your family and friends might know a lot of details about you, but not even the closest one of them knows how many hairs are on your head. God cares about everything in His creation, even the tiniest of birds, but He knows and loves people most of all—and that definitely includes you!

Jesus, thank You for teaching me that God knows me even better than I know myself and loves me like crazy. Help me to focus on that truth and never forget it! Amen.

Day 270

Shove Off!

Throw off your old sinful nature and your former way of life, which is corrupted by lust and deception. Instead, let the Spirit renew your thoughts and attitudes. Put on your new nature, created to be like God—truly righteous and holy.

EPHESIANS 4:22–24 NLT

Our old sinful nature loves to deceive us. It corrupts our minds with lies like "I can't do it. I'm not good enough." Throw off that thought as soon as it hits your brain! Let the Spirit renew your mind. Put on your new nature. Speak truth to yourself about who you are in Christ: "I can do all things through Christ, because he gives me strength" (Philippians 4:13 NCV).

The old sinful nature gets insecure and thinks, "No one really likes me. I'm unloved." Shove that thought into the trash! Think your new thought: The Lord says, "I have loved you. . .with an everlasting love" (Jeremiah 31:3 NLT).

Your old nature wants to steal your confidence. Choose to throw off those deceitful, destructive thoughts and attitudes, and renew your mind with truth!

Spirit, help me toss those old attitudes and renew my thoughts with truth.

Day 271

Listen Carefully

"If you listen carefully to what he says and do all that I say, I will be an enemy to your enemies and will oppose those who oppose you."
EXODUS 23:22 NIV

God sent an angel to help the Israelites. He told the Israelites to listen to the angel. If they did, God would take care of them. Today, we may not have an angel to guide the way but we have His Word. We have the Holy Spirit. The same promise holds true: "If you listen to My words and do what I say, I will take care of you."

That doesn't mean bad things won't happen. We live in a broken world where people make poor choices and things get messed up. But by staying close to God, we ensure that He's on our side. He loves His children, and He will take care of us.

I want to listen to You and do what You say, Father. I trust You to take care of me.

Day 272

You Don't Have to Fight Alone

Lord, battle with those who battle with me.
Fight against those who fight against me.
Psalm 35:1 NCV

When you face conflict in your life, whether it's a battle of wills or a battle of words, things can get intense. The fantastic news is you don't have to feel like you're facing all the conflict on your own. The Lord is on your side!

Examine your own heart and your motives when you're in the middle of a conflict. Ask God if there's any wrong in your life. If you know there is, confess it and ask for forgiveness, both from the Lord and the person you've offended.

When you feel like it's you against the world and you don't know what to do, ask the Lord for help. Ask Him to fight for you. You don't have to go through life all by yourself.

Lord, please fight against those people who are fighting against me. I need You!

Day 273

Praying for Offenders

If someone mistreats you because you are a Christian, don't curse him; pray that God will bless him.

Romans 12:14 TLB

Whoa! Sometimes we read scriptures that are hard to digest, and other times we read ones that feel impossible to walk out. For some, today's verse may feel that way in spades because it's asking us to pray for those who hurt us. When we've been wounded for being a believer, praying for God to bless the one who offended us usually isn't our default response. But friend, ask God to make it become just that.

Pray for the friend who mocks your faith. Pray for the boss who treats you badly for requesting Sundays off for church. Pray for the brother who picks on you relentlessly for reading the Bible. Pray for peers who make fun of you for praying before eating at lunchtime. Pray for the teammate who laughs because you listen to worship music rather than what's trendy. By doing this, you're choosing to love the unlovable. And God sees it.

Lord, please strengthen me to follow Your command to pray for my offenders. Amen.

Day 274

Overcome Evil with Good

Do not be overcome by evil, but overcome evil with good.
ROMANS 12:21 NASB

Hearing bad news or seeing a story about something tragic can quickly send us spiraling into a state of fear and panic. Sometimes it feels like the world is overrun by sadness, and it's easy to become overwhelmed by the presence of hardship. Before you fall into complete despair, though, look at the tools God's given you to fight evil: goodness, kindness, prayer, and love.

Your commitment to kindness brings light into the darkness. Darkness can't exist where the light shines because the light overpowers it. An act of kindness is a sign to the world that hope exists.

Father God, let Your light shine through the darkness! Give me opportunities to fight evil with my attitude and actions. I want to live a life of love, kindness, and goodness.

Day 275

A Rich Man and Jesus

"Good Teacher, what must I do to inherit eternal life?". . . "I've obeyed all these commandments since I was young." Looking at the man, Jesus felt genuine love for him. "There is still one thing you haven't done," he told him. "Go and sell all your possessions and give the money to the poor, and you will have treasure in heaven. Then come, follow me." At this the man's face fell, and he went away sad, for he had many possessions. Jesus looked around and said to his disciples, "How hard it is for the rich to enter the Kingdom of God!"

MARK 10:17, 20–23 NLT

This rich man loved to obey God's commandments and had a desire to know Jesus, but he wasn't willing to truly follow, obey, and believe Jesus because he wanted to hold on to his wealth, not give it up when Jesus asked. If we truly love Jesus as our Savior, we give up anything we have if Jesus asks us, because we know that no possession or wealth here on earth compares to the love and salvation He offers.

Jesus, help me to always be willing to give up everything and obey You no matter what. Amen.

Day 276

Love Your Enemies

"But to you who are listening I say: Love your enemies, do good to those who hate you, bless those who curse you, pray for those who mistreat you."

Luke 6:27–28 NIV

Jesus said these words to a big crowd. They were curious about what this teacher—who claimed to be God's Son—had to say. Many of them grew up in religious homes where they were taught to sacrifice animals, give money to the temple, and follow the rules. But Jesus took things further. He said we have to love the people who are hard to love.

That's more difficult than following a set of rules. Jesus knew that hate destroys us. It makes us angry and bitter. Love gives us life. By doing the hard thing and loving those who hate you, you point them to Christ and invite God's peace into your life.

This is a hard command, Lord. Help me love those who hate me, be kind to those who are mean, and pray for those who are cruel.

Day 277

Let Him Lead

"Follow me," Jesus said to him, and Levi got up, left everything and followed him.

LUKE 5:27–28 NIV

All the female needs to know in ballroom dancing is the basic step. That's it! Your partner does all the work. If you can follow his signals, he'll guide you across the floor like you're a pro. But that's the tricky part for us girls—it's not always easy to follow! Lack of trust makes us stiff. We take control by resisting our partner's cues and not moving where he wants us to go. We don't glide across the floor. Instead, the dance becomes a battle.

Jesus has called us to follow Him. Do you let Him lead? Or do you fight for control and push to move in a certain direction? Be confident in your partner, and relax into the dance! When we let go of fear and control and move in trust with Jesus, following Him becomes smooth, peaceful, and beautiful.

Jesus, trusting You feels scary sometimes. Build my confidence in You so I know You won't let me trip and fall. Help me let go of control and follow You wherever You lead.

Day 278

Meeting in the Moment

When others are happy, be happy with them.
If they are sad, share their sorrow.
ROMANS 12:15 TLB

One important way you can choose to love others is to meet them in the moment. Whether it's a sad or happy situation, just being present sends a powerful message that they matter to you. Don't be afraid to share their sorrow—instead be willing to sit in it with them. And when there's reason to celebrate, be quick to rejoice with them too! What a privilege to be part of another's life in such ways.

Who in your group of friends needs your support right now? Is there a family member who could use some cheering on? Do you know of someone needing to be championed as they take the next step? Embrace every opportunity to connect with others in meaningful ways. God created community for believers, and it's important to not only enjoy it but also contribute as well. Ask Him to open your eyes and ears to see and hear the needs of those around you. And then step out in faith, linking arms in beautiful and mighty moments.

Lord, help me meet others in their moments. Amen.

Day 279

Fiery Anger

And don't stay angry. Don't go to bed angry.
Don't give the Devil that kind of foothold in your life.
EPHESIANS 4:26–27 MSG

Did you know that if a building catches on fire, the fire spreads slower if all the doors inside are closed? Open doors allow the fire easy access into all areas of the structure.

Staying angry is like leaving doors open for temptation and sin to enter freely. When anger is present, retaliation, hatred, and bitterness are never far behind.

If we close the door to anger, the temptation to sin won't spread into our lives as quickly. It might hover outside the door, but it'll give us fair warning of its presence, allowing us time to plan our escape.

> Sometimes I can't find the "off switch" to my anger, God. Please give me the ability to close the door on my anger today!

Day 280

No Fear

[Jesus said:] "Don't be afraid of those who threaten you. For the time is coming when everything that is covered will be revealed, and all that is secret will be made known to all. . . . Don't be afraid of those who want to kill your body; they cannot touch your soul. Fear only God, who can destroy both soul and body in hell."

MATTHEW 10:26, 28 NLT

Jesus taught us to have no fear. Evil people and evil plans will be uncovered eventually. Above all, God sees and will bring consequences and justice. Keep praying to Him to do that and for wisdom about how to be strong against enemies, for protection, and for courage!

Jesus, remind me every day that I don't need to be afraid of anyone. You see and know all; You protect and provide; and You will make everything right in Your perfect timing. I fear and respect You alone. You are my Savior, and I know how much You love me. Amen.

Day 281

Help Me Love Them

Do not gloat when your enemy falls;
when they stumble, do not let your heart rejoice.
PROVERBS 24:17 NIV

When someone has been unkind or has hurt us, we want bad things to happen to them. But that's not how God operates. After all, we hurt Him each time we sin. But He loves us beyond measure, and His heart breaks when we're hurting. He wants our love for others to look like His love for each of us.

When someone who has hurt you has a bad day, go out of your way to be kind. They may not understand it, but it will make them wonder what makes you different. They may eventually figure out that you are God's child. Your choice to love someone who hurt you may be the thing that brings them to Christ.

Give me compassion for the people who hurt me, Lord. It won't come easily for me, but I want to honor You. Help me love them with Your love.

Day 282

Wrangling Resentment

But the snake said to the woman, "You will not die. God knows that if you eat the fruit from that tree, you will learn about good and evil and you will be like God!"

Genesis 3:4–5 NCV

That sting of jealousy—you know exactly what it feels like. She has it *all*, and it's Just. Not. Fair. Jealousy, if not checked, easily transforms into resentment. You start thinking God loves *her* and not you. God is blessing *him* and not you. Really what it boils down to is this: You think God is not fair. He doesn't love you.

That's how Satan tricked Eve too. He twisted God's command so Eve felt like God was withholding something from her. Instead of seeing God's command as her protection, Eve grew resentful. "Why is God keeping this from me? He's not loving! I should have this so I can be wise." Her resentment gave birth to sin. Where is your jealousy leading you?

Loving Father, forgive me for resenting You. You only want what's best for me. Help me recognize the lies about You and trust Your ways are right.

Day 283

So Deep, So High

Lord, your love reaches to the heavens, your loyalty to the skies. Your goodness is as high as the mountains. Your justice is as deep as the great ocean.

Psalm 36:5–6 NCV

No matter where you are right now, take a look outside and find some part of creation that amazes you. Is it how high the sky is? Is it the moon and the stars at night? Do you admire the leaves on trees or a stunning sunset?

God made all of those parts of creation. And just like they're so immense and more detailed than you'll ever realize, they also do a fantastic job of showing God's love for you. He loves you so much it's like His love reaches to the heavens. His loyalty and faithfulness stretch to the sky. His goodness is as powerful and as tall as mountains. And His justice is deep like the ocean depths. Soak in all of that love and loyalty and goodness and justice, and praise Him!

Lord, I praise You! There is no one and not a thing like You. Your power, might, and love astonish me.

Day 284

Blessed Loyalty

But Ruth said, "Do not urge me to leave you or to return from following you. For where you go I will go, and where you lodge I will lodge. Your people shall be my people, and your God my God."
Ruth 1:16 ESV

The book of Ruth tells us the story of Ruth (not too surprising) and her mother-in-law, Naomi. After Ruth's husband died, she was free to go back to her family, remarry, and live her own life. Ruth wasn't an Israelite like Naomi, and staying with her meant continuing into a foreign land and unknown circumstances.

Instead of leaving, though, Ruth stayed with Naomi. Even though Ruth and Naomi differed in many ways, Ruth trusted God and wanted to stay with His people. Because of her loyalty to God and His people, Ruth ended up marrying an Israelite named Boaz, and she became an ancestor of Jesus.

Dear God, make me someone who's loyal to You and Your people, even if it means venturing into unknown territory.

Day 285

Our Job

Do not take revenge, my dear friends, but leave room for God's wrath, for it is written: "It is mine to avenge; I will repay," says the Lord. On the contrary: "If your enemy is hungry, feed him; if he is thirsty, give him something to drink. In doing this, you will heap burning coals on his head."

Romans 12:19–20 NIV

Our job, while we're here, is to love God and others. That's it. It's *His* job to judge. It's *His* job to punish people. It's fine to agree with what God says in His Word about right and wrong—that's not judging. That's just admitting we understand what God says. But we're always, only supposed to treat others with love, compassion, and kindness. God will take care of discipline.

Judges and law enforcement officers handle the earthly consequences of people's actions. But they should always treat people with kindness and decency—even criminals. It's important to let God do His job. We're responsible for our job—to love.

Forgive me for judging others, Lord.
Help me love them instead.

Day 286

Worrywart

I tell you not to worry about your life. Don't worry about having something to eat, drink, or wear. Isn't life more than food or clothing? Look at the birds in the sky! They don't plant or harvest. They don't even store grain in barns. Yet your Father in heaven takes care of them. Aren't you worth much more than birds? Can worry make you live longer?
MATTHEW 6:25–27 CEV

Life is full of worries. *Do I look pretty enough? Am I going to do well on my test? Will my parents divorce? Will I ever marry?* Thoughts and fears about the future can be overwhelming. *College? Career? I have no idea!!! How am I supposed to know?* But Jesus tells us to take a deep breath and just stop—stop the worry, stop the racing thoughts, stop focusing on the problem and put your eyes on Him. Let it go. He's got this.

Lord, I give You all my worries—from the little things to the big things. You will provide. Fill me with Your peace and joy as I let go and trust You.

Day 287

So Much More

Simon said to Him, "Teacher, we have worked all night and we have caught nothing. But because You told me to, I will let the net down." When they had done this, they caught so many fish, their net started to break. They called to their friends working in the other boat to come and help them. They came and both boats were so full of fish they began to sink.

LUKE 5:5–7 NLV

Jesus' disciples had just spent the whole night fishing and had caught nothing, but Jesus only had to say the words and suddenly they caught loads of fish—enough to tear their nets and sink their boats! Never forget that Jesus is able to bless you with so much more than you expect. Keep learning about Him, trusting Him, praising Him, waiting on His perfect timing, and asking Him for everything you need. He just might provide so much more than you ever dreamed possible!

Jesus, help me to remember how You love to bless people–including me–in above-and-beyond kinds of ways! Amen.

Day 288

Confident in Community

Work happily together. Don't try to act big. Don't try to get into the good graces of important people, but enjoy the company of ordinary folks. And don't think you know it all!

Romans 12:16 TLB

Humility is important to God. Scripture says that it's pride that goes before the fall, so we need to stay grounded in the truth of who we are…and who we are not. When we embrace who God created us to be, we're choosing to love ourselves. Not in a prideful way but in a grateful way. We're letting Him know we like our skills and talents. It's saying we appreciate the gifts baked into us. And it's recognizing that we were made on purpose and for a purpose.

Friend, let confidence guide you into community. Be happy to bring your God-given abilities and hard-earned areas of expertise to the group. Be willing to work with others, not concerned about status or popularity. And recognize all that others bring into the mix too. This is a recipe for working happily together, and it delights God's heart.

Lord, help me choose to love myself so I'm confident and not conceited. Amen.

Day 289

God's Precious Love

How precious is Your mercy, God! And the sons of mankind take refuge in the shadow of Your wings.

Psalm 36:7 NASB

Did you know that an eagle's wingspan can reach upward of eight feet long? That means, when an eagle fully stretches its wings, it's taller than most professional basketball players.

Eagles don't just use their wings for flying. They also use them to provide protection to their young. The mama eagle spreads her wings over her young to shield them from snow, rain, and predators.

In His precious loving-kindness, God has enveloped you, His daughter, in the shadow of His wings.

> Dear heavenly Father, You are my only true source of refuge. Shelter me in the shadow of Your wings.

Day 290

Hang In There

For this light momentary affliction is preparing for us an eternal weight of glory beyond all comparison, as we look not to the things that are seen but to the things that are unseen. For the things that are seen are transient, but the things that are unseen are eternal.

2 CORINTHIANS 4:17–18 ESV

It's easy to misunderstand Christianity. Trust God, and everything will be okay. Trust God, and He will bless you beyond measure. Those things are true, but that doesn't mean we won't have problems. Sometimes the problems are enormous, and we don't know how we'll find our way to the other side.

But we will get through because God will never leave us. He will show us the way, and He will walk with us on the journey. He will bless those who live for Him even when it's hard. And one day we will look back and say, "It was all worth it."

What I'm going through right now doesn't feel "light," Father. Help me through this. Hold my hand and don't let go.

Day 291

Fashion Focused

"Has anyone by fussing in front of the mirror ever gotten taller by so much as an inch? All this time and money wasted on fashion—do you think it makes that much difference? Instead of looking at the fashions, walk out into the fields and look at the wildflowers. They never primp or shop, but have you ever seen color and design quite like it? . . . If God gives such attention to the appearance of wildflowers—most of which are never even seen—don't you think he'll attend to you, take pride in you, do his best for you?"

MATTHEW 6:27–30 MSG

God is a master artist—painting sunsets, sculpting canyons, and forming *you*. Of everything God has created, *you* are God's masterpiece—just as you are, without makeup, curling irons, and trendy clothes. Do you see yourself that way? Enjoying fashion is okay, but God sees past the clothes to who He made you to be. Don't nitpick all your imperfections, but celebrate the unique person you are.

Father, thank You for making me *me*.
Help me not to focus on things that don't matter.
Help me be confident in the way You shaped me.

Day 292

Wonderful Things

"Lord, you have done this wonderful thing for my sake and because you wanted to. You have made known all these great things."

1 Chronicles 17:19 NCV

Throughout King David's life, God led and protected him. David went from shepherding sheep to shepherding the Israelites as their king. All through his life, the Lord blessed him and also promised great blessings to David's descendants. David responded by praising God and acknowledging all the wonderful things He had done.

Like David, when you see the Lord working in your life and you recognize the ways He blesses you, praise Him! Acknowledge that God is the one who does wonderful things for your sake. It's nothing you've done on your own. Rather, it's because God has wanted to bless you in this way.

Lord, You have done so many wonderful things for my sake simply because You wanted to. Thank You! I praise You for Your greatness and wonderful generosity.

Day 293

Sleeping in Safety

I go to bed and sleep in peace, because, Lord, only you keep me safe.
Psalm 4:8 NCV

If you have trouble falling asleep, it's a perfect opportunity to pray. You can toss and turn while thinking over your day and thanking God for all the good that happened, but also ask Him for help with everything that's troubling you. If you're still awake, even after you've thanked Him for His blessings, remind yourself of some of His promises. One promise is that He will keep you safe. With His safety, you can go to bed and sleep in peace. You don't have to worry.

When worries do pop into your mind, give them over to the Lord. And keep giving them over to Him until you feel at peace.

Lord, thank You for keeping me safe! I am so grateful I can go to bed and sleep in peace because of You and Your constant protection.

Day 294

Match Your Words and Actions

Let's not merely say that we love each other;
let us show the truth by our actions.
1 JOHN 3:18 NLT

Do you ever observe people saying nice things but then doing nasty things? We're all guilty of that sometimes, and we need to be careful that we live honest lives—matching what we say with what we do. What Jesus says *always* matches what He does. His words are *always* true. He didn't just say He loves us; He proved His great love for all people with action. Romans 5:8 (NLV) says, "God showed His love to us. While we were still sinners, Christ died for us."

Jesus, I want to keep on learning from Your love, Your words, and Your actions. Please help my life to be a lot like Yours. I want to love not just in words but in everything I do.

Day 295

Messing Up

"You will say to them, 'This is what the Lord says: "Do men fall and not get up again? Does one turn away and not return?"'"

Jeremiah 8:4 NLV

Have you ever messed up? We all have. Even those who love God with their whole hearts and live to please Him will have a bad day now and then. We get grumpy. We snap at others. We may do a lot worse.

God knows we'll mess up. Like the verse says, He knows we will fall. The important thing after a fall is to get back up again. Tell God you're sorry. Make amends with people you've hurt. Then get back on track, loving God and loving others. We serve a gracious, loving God, and He always forgives us when we're sincerely sorry.

I'm so sorry for my mistakes, Lord. I'm sorry for my bad attitude and the poor choices I've made. Please forgive me. I want to get back on track and live for You.

Day 296

Overconfidence

Trust in the Lord with all your heart. Never rely on what you think you know. . . . Never let yourself think that you are wiser than you are.

Proverbs 3:5, 7 GNT

You're a teenager now! You have *all* the answers, right? You don't need your parents telling you what to do—you've got it figured out. Every teenager on the planet is tempted to think that. As we grow in independence, it's natural to start pushing away from our parents. But there's wisdom in not being overconfident in yourself. Your parents and other adults have a lot more experience than you, and the lessons they share are worth paying attention to.

Overconfidence makes you believe you are strong, capable, and brave and don't need anyone's help. Overconfidence is simply pride, and that's a sin. True confidence means having the wisdom and humility to place your trust where it belongs—first, in Jesus, and also in other trustworthy adults who can help guide you. How are you overconfident? How is God prompting you to show humility and true confidence?

Lord, forgive me for my pride. Help me be humble and teachable and listen to the wisdom of others.

Day 297

Loving Through Tough Conversations

Never pay back evil for evil. Do things in such a way that everyone can see you are honest clear through.

Romans 12:17 TLB

If you're committed to choosing love, then there is no place for revenge. There's no room for dishonesty. Because anything that hurts another isn't motivated by genuine compassion, pure and simple. In your opinion, there may be justification for your anger. There may be a well-concocted strategy to hide your true motivation. But love is kind and doesn't dishonor others. It keeps no record of wrongs nor does it delight in evil. Instead, it rejoices in the truth.

Friend, love others enough to be honest. If they've hurt you or treated you poorly, talk about it with them. Share your feelings. Explain how their actions frustrated you. Care enough to try to work through disagreements, believing they want the same. Sometimes choosing to love others means you have tough conversations in the hope of reconciliation.

Lord, thank You for reminding me that honest conversations rather than vengeful plans reveal my love for those in my life. Amen.

Day 298

Outside the Comfort Zone

"Which of these three do you think was a neighbor to the man who fell into the hands of robbers?" The expert in the law replied, "The one who had mercy on him." Jesus told him, "Go and do likewise."

Luke 10:36–37 NIV

Sometimes people look for excuses to get out of things they know they're supposed to do, which is what the experts in the Law were doing here.

They'd just asked Jesus, "Who is my neighbor?" hoping He'd tell them their neighbors were friends and family. They didn't want to leave their comfort zone in order to fulfill God's command to love thy neighbor.

Instead, Jesus told them about the good Samaritan, a social outcast who showed compassion to a stranger in need. Jesus wants us to be a neighbor to everyone and show mercy to anyone in need, not just to family and friends.

Dear Jesus, I know it's important to step outside my comfort zone and show mercy to those in need. Make me a good neighbor to everyone, not just those I feel comfortable around.

Day 299

Watch Out!

[Jesus said:] Watch out for false prophets! They dress up like sheep, but inside they are wolves who have come to attack you. You can tell what they are by what they do. . . . You can tell who the false prophets are by their deeds.

MATTHEW 7:15–16, 20 CEV

Jesus warned strongly against false prophets and teachers for good reason. There are some really confusing differences among churches and people who call themselves Christians. Some differences are no big deal because they're just a matter of traditions and preferences. But some differences result from churches, teachers, and preachers going against the Word of God. Second Corinthians 11:13 (CEV) says these false teachers "only pretend to be apostles of Christ." Jesus is not surprised by these false teachers and churches, so we don't have to be afraid. If we keep ourselves strongly dependent on Jesus and the Bible through the Holy Spirit, He will help us figure out the false teachers and churches from those who truly know, love, and serve Him and preach the *whole* Word of God.

Jesus, please keep me on the lookout for false prophets and teachers, and help me avoid them. I want to hear what You want to teach me, straight from Your Word and Your leading! Amen.

Day 300

He Always Forgives

A man who is right with God falls seven times,
and rises again, but the sinful fall in time of trouble.
Proverbs 24:16 NLV

Being a Christian doesn't mean we're perfect. Far from it! We still mess up. We're human, and we're going to say and do things we regret. But those who truly love Christ will always do their best to make things right as soon as they realize what they've done.

The great news is, there's nothing we can do to cause God to stop loving us. He adores us! No matter what we've done or how far we've strayed from Him, we can always come back. He'll be right there, waiting with open arms to welcome us home.

Thank You for always forgiving me and always welcoming me back, Father. Keep me close to You. When I'm tempted to stray, pull me back into Your safety. Help me learn from my mistakes, and keep me close to You.

Day 301

Shine, Girl!

"You are like light for the whole world. . . . No one lights a lamp and puts it under a bowl; instead it is put on the lampstand, where it gives light for everyone in the house. In the same way your light must shine before people, so that they will see the good things you do and praise your Father in heaven."

MATTHEW 5:14–16 GNT

Peer pressure is real. You want to fit in and be accepted. No one likes to stand out and set themselves up for teasing and bullying. Yet following Jesus means going against the flow. You're going to stand out—and you're supposed to. But sometimes we like to slip that bowl over our light and kinda hide it a bit, you know? Here's the thing: Darkness *needs* the light. Your school, your social circle, your community *needs* the light you have. Push back against the darkness and let your light shine!

Lord, forgive me for being afraid sometimes to let my light shine. Give me courage and boldness to stand for You so others can see You and find You.

Day 302

So Sad

Hannah was so sad that she cried and prayed to the LORD. She made a promise, saying, "LORD All-Powerful, see how sad I am. Remember me and don't forget me. If you will give me a son, I will give him back to you all his life."

1 SAMUEL 1:10–11 NCV

For years, Hannah was heartbroken because she wasn't a mom. One year, as she prayed and cried in the house of the Lord, she made a promise she meant to keep. If only God would remember her and give her a son, Hannah promised to give the baby back to the Lord.

God answered Hannah's prayers and blessed her with a baby. When her son was old enough, Hannah took him to live in the house of the Lord.

Just like Hannah could cry and come to the Lord in her sadness, you can too! You always can pray, no matter how sad you feel.

Lord All-Powerful, You remember me even when I'm sad. You won't ever forget me.

Day 303

God's Heart for Harmony

Don't quarrel with anyone. Be at peace with everyone, just as much as possible.

Romans 12:18 TLB

Having fights and disagreements with people is a normal part of life. We each have our own ideas and opinions about how to move forward. And like everyone else, we feel confident our ways are the best ways. So how could we not quarrel from time to time? We are imperfect people, living in an imperfect world, with other imperfect people. There's no way around it.

The challenge is to balance our irritation with a desire for peace. It doesn't mean we stuff feelings, but maybe we don't have to be offended at every turn either. What if we asked God to help us know when to share our frustrations and when to let them go? And what if we asked for a heart bent toward peaceful resolutions rather than exasperated exchanges? We need the Lord's help to love family and friends well. We need His help to seek harmony with classmates, teammates, and coworkers. Friend, we need God's heart for harmony every day.

Lord, give me a desire to be at peace as much as possible. Amen.

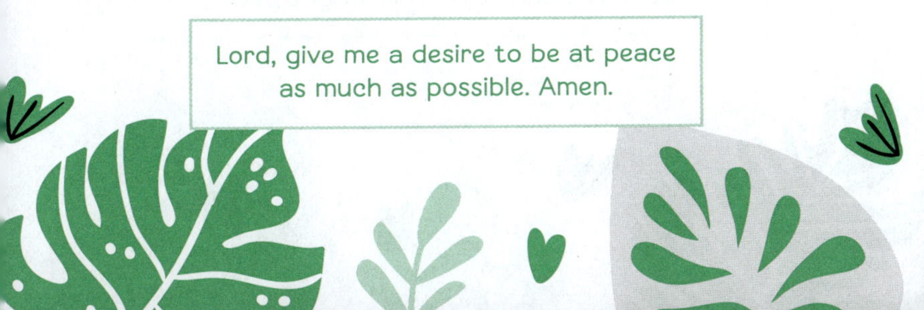

Day 304

Rejoice in Discipline

"For the Lord *disciplines those he loves,*
and he punishes each one he accepts as his child."
Hebrews 12:6 NLT

If you've faced the consequences for something you've done wrong, then rejoice! This means the Lord has adopted you as His daughter and is keeping you on the path of righteousness.

Praise God and thank Him for loving you enough to correct you. After all, what good parent lets a child continue in destructive behavior? A good mother or father won't allow their child to keep playing in the street when cars are coming, even if that child wants nothing more than to stay in the street.

Discipline doesn't always feel loving at the time, but God sees the bigger picture and allows a little bit of temporary discomfort to save His children from eternal agony.

Dear God, it's hard to be thankful for discipline, but I'm grateful You love me enough to reveal and punish my sins. Help me learn from Your discipline and stay on the right path.

Day 305

Drastic Change

Saul was still breathing out murderous threats against the Lord's disciples. . . . As he neared Damascus on his journey, suddenly a light from heaven flashed around him. He fell to the ground and heard a voice say to him, "Saul, Saul, why do you persecute me?"

Acts 9:1, 3–4 NIV

Saul had a dramatic experience when Jesus stopped him in his tracks and completely turned his life around. He went from hating and hunting down Christians to being Jesus' chosen instrument to spread His truth and love. (Read on in Acts 9 to get the full story.) It's truly miraculous and amazing what Jesus can do to change people drastically. Don't forget how Jesus can keep working in your life to turn around any difficult situation, and He can change the heart of any person you know who still needs to choose Him as Savior. So keep praying and trusting!

Lord, I believe You still work in dramatic, miraculous ways today to change people and help them choose You.

Day 306

The Lion

We are pressed on every side, but we still have room to move. We are often in much trouble, but we never give up. People make it hard for us, but we are not left alone. We are knocked down, but we are not destroyed.

2 CORINTHIANS 4:8–9 NLV

Christ is almighty. He's all-powerful. When we accept Him as Savior, He lives in us. That means we have access to all that power! No matter what we face, we'll come out on the other side still standing. Like Rocky Balboa, we may get banged and bruised up a bit, but we won't be destroyed. In the end, we'll be the victor.

What do you face right now? Whatever it is, remember Christ is stronger. He is called the Lion of Judah. He lives in you, fights for you, and gives you the strength to face another day. Hold your head up. Picture Him as a lion walking beside you, protecting you, and keeping you from being destroyed.

Thank You for walking with me and giving me strength. Let me feel Your presence, Lord.

Day 307

Girl of Grace

[Love] is not easily angered, it keeps no record of wrongs.
1 Corinthians 13:5 NIV

The awkward friendship dance can really hit your insecurities. Are we friends. . .or not? You might be texting up a frenzy with someone, then all of a sudden it's total silence. You start questioning yourself. *Did I do something wrong? Why doesn't she like me? What's wrong with me?*

Navigating relationships can be *so* tricky, not to mention emotionally exhausting. Kick your insecurities to the curb and stay confident in yourself by *choosing* not to be easily angered. Was that supposed to be a slight? Choose to overlook it and not let it bother you. Feeling the cold shoulder? Choose not to take it personally. Maybe she's just really busy. Even if you *know* something was meant as a dig, you can choose to brush it off. By showing grace instead of taking offense, your friendships will remain strong—and you'll feel a lot more secure too!

Lord, help me not to read into things and take offense where maybe it wasn't intended. Help me show grace to my friends, just as You show grace to me.

Day 308

Sharing It All

All my longings lie open before you, Lord; my sighing is not hidden from you. My heart pounds, my strength fails me; even the light has gone from my eyes. My friends and companions avoid me because of my wounds; my neighbors stay far away.

Psalm 38:9–11 NIV

It can be tempting to keep your feelings to yourself. While it's very wise to not share all your thoughts and feelings with everyone, it's a really great choice to share your hopes, dreams, thoughts, and ideas with the Lord. After all, He knows you completely. He knows your longings. He knows your frustrations and disappointments. He knows when you're sad and when you're tired. He knows when it feels like you've lost all the pep in your step.

Even if and when other people avoid you, the Lord won't turn away. Rather, the Lord will draw near. All you need to do is draw near to Him.

Lord, You know all I want and all I need. You know what happens on my worst days and on my best days. I am so grateful that I have You.

Day 309

The Ultimate Kindness

"For God so loved the world, that He gave His only Son, so that everyone who believes in Him will not perish, but have eternal life."

JOHN 3:16 NASB

Our limited human brain will never fully grasp the splendor and majesty of our perfect, eternal, and holy God. Similarly, we'll never completely wrap our minds around how serious, revolting, and hurtful our sins are to God.

When sin entered the world, God could've removed Himself and left humanity to suffer alone. But God loved the world so much that He gave His only Son to take the punishment we deserved so we could be restored to right standing with Him.

When we understand the holiness of God and the horror of sin, we see the incredible mercy, compassion, and kindness shown to us in what Jesus did on the cross. What's more, God made this ultimate kindness open to all who confess their sin and claim Jesus as their Savior.

Thank You for sending Your Son to take the punishment for our sins, God! What an incredible gift You've given the world.

Day 310

Too Wonderful to Be Measured

I want you to know all about Christ's love, although it is too wonderful to be measured. Then your lives will be filled with all that God is. I pray that Christ Jesus and the church will forever bring praise to God. His power at work in us can do far more than we dare ask or imagine.

Ephesians 3:19–21 CEV

The love of Jesus is so wonderful, so above and beyond, so much bigger than anything that anyone can ever measure or even possibly imagine, and He is able to do so much more than our very best hopes and dreams! As you pray and ask for His blessings and help in every area of your life, think about how great His love for you is and how His plans for your life are always the best.

Jesus, thank You for Your endless, immeasurable, awesome love and power in my life! Amen.

Day 311

He's Working

He lifted me out of the pit of despair, out of the mud and the mire. He set my feet on solid ground and steadied me as I walked along. He has given me a new song to sing, a hymn of praise to our God. Many will see what he has done and be amazed. They will put their trust in the LORD.

PSALM 40:2–3 NLT

Sometimes our circumstances can get so bad that we don't see how things will ever get better. We call that place "the pit." God is no stranger to pits. He's been lifting His children out of them since the beginning of time. He knows exactly where you are and what you're going through, and He's working right now to get you to a better place.

Sometimes He lets us know what He's doing. More often, we just have to trust that He's working, even though we can't see results as quickly as we'd like. No matter what, keep believing. Keep calling out to Him. He is already on His way, and He's got something great in store for your life, sooner than you think.

I trust You, Lord. Please hurry.

Day 312

You Do You

In those days Israel had no king; all the people did whatever seemed right in their own eyes.

JUDGES 21:25 NLT

Our culture has abandoned truth. The world tells us that biological sex doesn't matter—you can choose whatever gender (or nongender) you want to be. You can choose whatever gender you're sexually attracted to—or both! These and many other lies are accepted—even celebrated. Diving into this issue can be very complex and should be treated carefully and lovingly. Yet we also cannot abandon God's truth.

Our culture has rejected Jesus as King (Romans 1:21–32). But we have the Spirit of truth who guides us (John 16:13). Speaking the truth is not popular—it didn't win Jesus any points with the crowd either. But Jesus had the courage to love people *and* stand for truth at the same time. How do you need to follow Jesus' example?

Spirit of Truth, please guide me in what is right. King Jesus, please give me courage to stand for truth. Help me to find the balance of loving others, yet not compromising my beliefs.

Day 313

How to Delight the Lord

The Lord directs the steps of the godly. He delights in every detail of their lives. Though they stumble, they will never fall, for the Lord holds them by the hand.

Psalm 37:23–24 NLT

This verse says God "delights" in every detail of a Christian's life. When God delights in someone, it means He is pleased with them. They make His heart happy. So. . .what does it take to delight the Lord?

Obedience. Trust. Faith. Loving Him and loving others. He doesn't require perfection. He's fully aware that we're human and that we're going to mess up. But He looks for people who love Him with all their hearts and who sincerely try to live for Him. When He sees someone like that, He keeps a special eye on them, whispering guidance and wisdom into their hearts and making their path smooth.

I need You to guide my steps, Lord.
Help me live in a way that pleases You.

Day 314

Guidance and Direction

Then he prayed, "LORD, God of my master Abraham, make me successful today, and show kindness to my master Abraham. See, I am standing beside this spring, and the daughters of the townspeople are coming out to draw water. May it be that when I say to a young woman, 'Please let down your jar that I may have a drink,' and she says, 'Drink, and I'll water your camels too'—let her be the one you have chosen for your servant Isaac. By this I will know that you have shown kindness to my master."

GENESIS 24:12–14 NIV

In Genesis, Abraham's servant was on a huge mission: finding a wife for Abraham's son, Isaac. Instead of just randomly choosing any woman, though, the servant prayed to God for guidance and direction.

Like Abraham's servant, ask God to help you when you're confused. When you have a big decision to make or a task to begin, pray for the Lord's help. Ask Him for success. He'll bring clarity in amazing ways.

Lord God, please make it abundantly obvious what I should do. Please grant me success!

Day 315

Let God Handle It

Dear friends, never avenge yourselves. Leave that to God, for he has said that he will repay those who deserve it. Don't take the law into your own hands.

ROMANS 12:19 TLB

God is very clear in His Word when He says for us to *not* take matters into our own hands. Plotting and planning revenge isn't for us to do. Your heavenly Father will manage in His own way and in His own time. So when someone deserves a rebuke, He promises to handle it. Friend, don't you see this as freedom?

Trusting God in these situations gives us breathing room. It's not up to us to figure out! We can choose love over retaliation. Compassion rather than vengeance. Kindness and not payback. And when you think about it, wouldn't you rather someone have to answer to the Lord over you anyway?

Lord, thank You for being my protector and the one to avenge on my behalf. Help me keep this perspective when someone hurts me in any way. I choose to love them and trust You. Amen.

Day 316

The Thief on the Cross

Then he said, "Jesus, remember me when you enter your kingdom."
He said, "Don't worry, I will. Today you will join me in paradise."
Luke 23:42–43 MSG

As Jesus hung on the cross, life slowly fading from Him, two thieves hung beside Him. One thief mocked Jesus, but the second thief realized he was hanging next to the Son of God and asked to be remembered in Jesus' kingdom.

Jesus promised the second thief that he'd see Him in paradise that same day. What comfort that must've brought to the thief as he took his final breaths!

Even while dying for the sins of mankind, Jesus showed mercy and kindness. The reason Jesus hung on the cross was for people just like the thief. By offering mercy to a dying common criminal, Jesus showed us it's never too late to realize He is King and accept the forgiveness He offers.

Dear Jesus, You are the Son of God and the only one who can forgive my sins. Thank You for what You did on the cross and for Your mercy and kindness to all.

Day 317

Give Your Way to Jesus

Be happy in the Lord. And He will give you the desires of your heart. Give your way over to the Lord. Trust in Him also. And He will do it. He will make your being right and good show as the light, and your wise actions as the noon day. Rest in the Lord and be willing to wait for Him.

Psalm 37:4–7 NLV

What does it mean to "give your way over to the Lord"? It means you say, "I don't want my own way, Jesus. I want Your way instead. Guide me on the good and right paths that You have planned for me." Ask Jesus to help you rest in Him and let your joy come from trusting Him. He gave you your life, and you can let Him lead it. He wants to bless you in the best kinds of ways, always.

Jesus, help me to want Your way in my life. I want all my happiness and joy to come from following You, resting in You, and waiting on You! Amen.

Day 318

Have Patience

Put on a heart of compassion, kindness, humility, gentleness, and patience; bearing with one another, and forgiving each other, whoever has a complaint against anyone; just as the Lord forgave you, so must you do also.

Colossians 3:12–13 NASB

We all mess up. We have bad days. We're grumpy or forgetful. When we have those days, we want others to have patience with us. We want them to be kind and gentle. We *don't* want them pointing out our mistakes or reminding us that we failed.

God treats us with kindness, compassion, and forgiveness, and that's how He wants us to treat others. Next time someone annoys you with their failures, ask yourself how you'd want to be treated in the same situation. Remind yourself that God is gracious and kind, and offer the same type of love to others.

Teach me to be patient with others, Lord.
Thank You for always being patient and kind to me.

Day 319

Good or Bad Influence?

It will be terrible for people who cause even one of my little followers to sin. Those people would be better off thrown into the deepest part of the ocean with a heavy stone tied around their necks!

MATTHEW 18:6 CEV

Loving parents protect their children from danger and harm. God, as our loving Father, fiercely guards His children as well. Causing another believer to sin is a very serious offense to God. Your words and actions matter. If your gossip leads another Christian to gossip, God is greatly displeased. If your prejudice causes you to exclude someone deemed "lesser" and your Christian friends follow your example, God will hold you accountable.

You can be certain your influence on others matters a great deal to God. He promises sobering consequences if our behavior leads another Christian to stumble into sin. Carefully examine your life. Are your words honoring Jesus? Would your actions make Jesus proud?

God, thank You for this reminder that my influence is a serious matter. Show me how I haven't been honoring You. Help me lead people toward You and not away from You.

Day 320

Seeing His Kind Faithfulness

Then the man bowed down and worshiped the Lord, saying, "Praise be to the Lord, the God of my master Abraham, who has not abandoned his kindness and faithfulness to my master."

Genesis 24:26–27 NIV

When Abraham's servant asked God for guidance and success, the Lord worked in amazing ways. Prayers were answered almost immediately, and the unbelievable became believable. The Lord led Abraham's servant to the absolutely perfect wife for Abraham's son Isaac.

After Abraham's servant saw the Lord at work, he didn't shrug it off. He bowed down and worshipped the Lord. He praised God because he recognized the Lord's kindness and faithfulness.

When you know the Lord has answered your prayer and has been kind and faithful to you, worship Him! Praise His holy name and thank Him for His faithful kindness.

Praise be to You, Lord! Thank You for Your kindness and faithfulness to me. I choose to worship You and You alone.

Day 321

Being Full of Compassion

Instead, feed your enemy if he is hungry. If he is thirsty give him something to drink and you will be "heaping coals of fire on his head." In other words, he will feel ashamed of himself for what he has done to you.

ROMANS 12:20 TLB

The perfect response when someone is treating you badly is to be kind. In a world where you can be anything, be full of compassion. You don't have to treat others the way they treat you, especially when it's awful. Instead, you can be the one to respond with a generous spirit. You can choose love.

This doesn't mean you're a weak person who can't stand up for herself. You're not being a doormat for others to walk all over. Instead, you're choosing to see the bigger picture. You're being the bigger person. And when you don't respond in kind, it gives God the opportunity to move in the heart of the one being hurtful to you. And He will honor your thoughtful choice.

Lord, please strengthen me to choose love when it feels hard to do. Amen.

Day 322

A Solitary Place to Pray

Very early in the morning, while it was still dark, Jesus got up, left the house and went off to a solitary place, where he prayed. Simon and his companions went to look for him, and when they found him, they exclaimed: "Everyone is looking for you!"

Mark 1:35–37 NIV

Even when Jesus had many things to do and many people wanting to see Him, hear Him, learn from Him, and be healed by Him, He took time to get away and pray. We need to remember this lesson daily—that if even Jesus, who was sinless and perfect, needed alone time to rest away from other people and spend time in prayer, how much more do we need that kind of time?

Jesus, help me to remember Your example of quiet, alone time and prayer. I don't want other responsibilities to get in the way of making You my priority. Help me to balance and prioritize my life well, with You first. Amen.

Day 323

Obey Your Parents

Children, obey your parents in the Lord, for this is right. Honor your father and mother (which is the first commandment with a promise), so that it may turn out well for you, and that you may live long on the earth.
Ephesians 6:1–3 nasb

When we're born, we're totally dependent on our parents to take care of us. The older we get, the more independent we become and the less we need them to meet our needs—until one day, we can leave home and take care of ourselves. As we journey toward independence, it's easy to get frustrated with our parents. We want different things than they do, and we don't always agree with them.

But God knew what He was doing. Even if you don't like their decisions, trust God. Obey Him by honoring and obeying your parents. This will please Him, and He will bless you.

Thank You for my parents, Lord. Help me honor and obey them, even when I don't want to. I want to honor You.

Day 324

Listen Up!

While Peter was talking, a bright cloud covered them.
A voice came from the cloud and said, "This is my Son,
whom I love, and I am very pleased with him. Listen to him!"
MATTHEW 17:5 NCV

"Listen to me!" How many times a week do you hear this from your parents? What does your mom *really* mean when she says that? She's not saying to mindlessly hear what she says and then forget—that's why you get in trouble! She means *understand* what she's saying and *obey*.

God the Father audibly commanded Peter, James, and John to truly listen to Jesus—to not just hear what He says but to seek to understand with a willingness to respond. God's command still echoes to us today: "Do not merely listen to the word, and so deceive yourselves. Do what it says" (James 1:22 NIV). How well do you listen to Jesus? When you read the Bible, are you seeking to understand what it says and obey its commands?

> Jesus, help me truly listen to You–not just mindlessly read my Bible or halfheartedly listen at church. Help me understand Your message and be willing to obey it.

Day 325

Are You There?

How long, LORD, must I call for help, but you do not listen? Or cry out to you, "Violence!" but you do not save?

HABAKKUK 1:2 NIV

It doesn't always feel like God hears your prayers. If you don't notice an answer to your prayers, you may wonder if He's listening at all.

God hears you. He listens to you. And He's answering your prayers. Because God is God and you're not, He hears and listens and answers in different ways than you expect or even understand.

Instead of getting frustrated if He's not doing everything you want Him to do, remember He won't magically fulfill your every desire. Instead of doubting His goodness or His love for you, wait for Him to show you His good purpose. It may take much longer than you might ever expect, but it doesn't mean He's not at work. Keep calling out to Him. Keep trusting He'll keep working in your life.

Lord, waiting is so difficult! Please help me wait patiently for You. In the meantime, please show me in some way, either little or big, that You hear me and that You're at work.

Day 326

The Gift of Faith

But a poor widow came and put in two very small copper coins, worth only a few cents. Calling his disciples to him, Jesus said, "Truly I tell you, this poor widow has put more into the treasury than all the others. They all gave out of their wealth; but she, out of her poverty, put in everything—all she had to live on."

MARK 12:42–44 NIV

One of the greatest gifts you can give to God is your faith. Two small coins might not seem like much, but the faith of a person who entrusts all they have to the Lord can make a big impact for the kingdom of God.

You may not think you have much to offer God, but it doesn't take lots of money or talent to serve Him. God can do more with a humble heart that says, "This is what I have, Lord; it's Yours," than He can with someone who has a million dollars and a hard heart.

Dear Jesus, everything I have belongs to You! Give me opportunities to glorify You with the gifts You've given me, even if they seem small to the world.

Day 327

The Spirit Is Willing, but the Body Is Weak

[Jesus said:] "Watch and pray so that you will not be tempted. Man's spirit is willing, but the body does not have the power to do it."
MATTHEW 26:41 NLV

Sometimes we have good intentions to do a good job with something, and then we just don't follow through. Can you relate? Do you ever plan to study really well for an upcoming test but then find yourself quickly cramming the night before? Do you ever plan to have regular time with Jesus, but you keep letting everything else in your life take priority over Him?

We are human, and we have struggles and temptations that keep us from doing the good things we should do and we intend to do. That's why we need to pray for help. We need to tell Jesus, "I can't do this on my own! Because of sin, I'm tempted to mess up all the time! I need Your great big power working in me to overcome this temptation."

Jesus, I can't do anything good without You! Please help me with everything! Amen.

Day 328

Listen to Your Parents

Listen, my son, to your father's instruction,
and do not ignore your mother's teaching.
PROVERBS 1:8 NASB

Most parents try to be good parents. They may make mistakes, but their instructions are often based on experience. They try to pass on things they've learned in life so you won't make the same mistakes they did.

When your parents give you advice, listen to it. Consider what they're saying and why they want you to know it. For example, they may have eaten a lot of junk food when they were young and now their bodies are paying the price in the form of aches and pains. Maybe they made poor choices in friendships and it landed them in trouble. Remember, they've lived longer and seen more. Listen to them.

Sometimes I don't want to listen to my parents. They seem out of touch. But I know they love me and want what's best for me. Help me honor them by listening to their advice.

Day 329

Know It, Speak It!

Jesus answered, "The Scriptures say: 'No one can live only on food. People need every word that God has spoken.'"
MATTHEW 4:4 CEV

Jesus was alone, hot, and HANGRY! He'd been fasting in the desert for forty days, and He was at the lowest of lows—which is right when the enemy likes to attack. Satan came along and started tempting Jesus, but Jesus knew how to fight. With every temptation, Jesus quoted scripture and didn't let Satan twist God's commands.

How well do you know your Bible? We can stand confidently when we are strong in God's Word. How much scripture is hidden in your heart? The more you feed your soul with God's truth, the more you'll recognize Satan's lies and tricks. And when you're feeling low and vulnerable, you'll have the weapons to fight against temptation. Find a scripture that's meaningful to you, and start memorizing it today!

Jesus, please help me know and memorize Your Word so I can stand confidently against the schemes of the enemy.

Day 330

Conquering Evil with Kindness

Don't let evil get the upper hand, but conquer evil by doing good.
ROMANS 12:21 TLB

Did you know that when you do good in the world, it helps conquer evil? In some situations, it may even help shut it down completely. When the new girl at school is treated poorly and feels unaccepted, your friendship changes everything. When your classmates treat the substitute teacher with disrespect but you show intentional kindness, it makes a difference in her day. Every time you refuse to gossip, evil loses. When you lead your team with compassion rather than cruelty, evil is shut down.

Today, ask God to open your eyes to see where you can conquer evil through goodness. Where can you shine Jesus into the world? How can you bring encouragement in bighearted ways? What friend or family member needs to be lavished with your love and support? Ask God to open your eyes to opportunities to defeat evil with kindness.

Lord, equip me to bring Your goodness into the lives of those around me so evil loses its power. Amen.

Day 331

Renewed Mercies

The faithful love of the LORD never ends! His mercies never cease. Great is his faithfulness; his mercies begin afresh each morning.

LAMENTATIONS 3:22–23 NLT

We all have days when we feel like we're failing at life. Maybe you can't handle the stress of school, you knock over everything you touch, and instead of extending kindness, you respond angrily over something small.

If you're discouraged, take heart! When you go to sleep at night, the Lord continues working in your heart. Come morning, He presents you with a brand-new day filled with fresh opportunities for love, kindness, and grace.

No matter how today went, no matter how far you fell short, tomorrow is a new day. The Lord's mercies are already there waiting for you.

I can't believe how much I fail sometimes, Lord Jesus. It's like I can't get anything right. Help me see Your daily mercies and remember that You're faithful even when I fail.

Day 332

Zacchaeus and Jesus

He was seeking to see who Jesus was.
Luke 19:3 ESV

Zacchaeus was a tax collector known for cheating and taking way too much of other people's money. But Zacchaeus was curious about Jesus and wanted to see Him as He traveled through Jericho. He wasn't very tall, so he ran ahead of where Jesus would walk and climbed a tree. Soon Jesus was near, and when He reached that tree, He stopped and spotted Zacchaeus. He called him by name and said, "Come down right away. I'm going to your house today." Zacchaeus climbed down immediately and welcomed Jesus to his home. As Zacchaeus spent time with Jesus, he was sorry for his sins. He wanted to give back to people all the money he had cheated them out of plus four times more.

Jesus, I'm thankful for the example of Zacchaeus, who was determined to get close to You and then admitted his sins and wanted to make things right. I want to be a lot like Zacchaeus. Amen.

Day 333

One Day

For I consider that the sufferings of this present time are not worthy to be compared with the glory that is to be revealed to us.
ROMANS 8:18 NASB

Life is hard. It's also filled with joy and happiness and good things. But when something hurts, it can hurt *a lot*. Unfortunately, suffering is just part of the journey.

But God's Word is filled with promises to His children. He will never leave us or turn His back on us. He loves to bless us. And one day, we will live with Him in heaven. When we get there, it will be so great, we won't even remember the suffering we endured here on earth.

For now, focus on all the ways God blesses you every single day. He sends things into your life just to make you smile—He loves you that much! And hold on to the promise that, one day, every tear will be wiped away forever.

Thank You for Your blessings now, Father, and for the promise that one day I'll live with You for eternity.

Day 334

Armor of God

Let the mighty strength of the Lord make you strong. Put on all the armor that God gives, so you can defend yourself against the devil's tricks. We are not fighting against humans. We are fighting against forces and authorities and against rulers of darkness and powers in the spiritual world. So put on all the armor that God gives. Then when that evil day comes, you will be able to defend yourself. And when the battle is over, you will still be standing firm.

EPHESIANS 6:10–13 CEV

A spiritual battle rages around you. Good news: God has already provided all the armor we need to survive this war—we just need to put it on! Bad news: Without activating this armor, we're easy targets for Satan. Good news: We're not playing offense; we're only playing defense. Bad news: We can't let our guard down; we must always be prepared to fight. Great news: Christ already won the victory! Now we must hold that territory. Stand firm!

Thank You, Lord, for equipping me for battle. Help me stand firm and not let Satan push me around. May Your mighty strength fill me and make me strong.

Day 335

Belt of Truth

So stand strong, with the belt of truth tied around your waist.

Ephesians 6:14 NCV

Belts keep our clothing in place. In the same way, God's armor hinges on truth. Without truth and trustworthiness, the other armor can't stay in place. We can't stand against the enemy if we're able to be deceived. We must internalize God's truth so we can recognize the enemy's lies. Do you hear Satan whisper that you're not good enough? Do sly thoughts enter your mind that no one really likes you? That you're a screwup? That God doesn't really care? Those are all lies straight from the pit of hell. Hold your ground! Don't let the enemy invade your thoughts and chip away at your relationships with God and others. Saturate yourself with God's Word and confidently stand against the enemy's deceit.

Lord, please reveal to me the lies I've accepted about myself and about You. In the name of Jesus, I rebuke those lies! Help me replace the lies with Your truth so I can stand strong and not give the enemy any kind of foothold in my life.

Day 336

Breastplate of Righteousness

Stand firm then. . .with the breastplate of righteousness in place.
Ephesians 6:14 NIV

"Righteousness" is "right living." Paul wrote, "Do not let any part of your body become an instrument of evil to serve sin. Instead, give yourselves completely to God, for you were dead, but now you have new life. So use your whole body as an instrument to do what is right for the glory of God" (Romans 6:13 NLT).

Is your tongue glorifying God with the words you say? Are your eyes glorifying God with the things you watch and read? Are your ears glorifying God with the things you listen to? Righteous living protects our hearts from the attacks of the enemy. When we choose not to put on our breastplate of righteousness—when we choose not to "live rightly" and follow God's ways—we become vulnerable to sin. Evaluate all the areas of your life. How do you need to start living right?

Lord, please forgive me for the ways I have not lived rightly before You. Help me wear the breastplate of righteousness so I can protect myself from temptations to sin.

Day 337

Shoes of Peace

For shoes, put on the peace that comes from the Good News so that you will be fully prepared.
EPHESIANS 6:15 NLT

We can confidently stand against the enemy when our feet are firmly grounded in the peace that comes from Jesus. He said, "Peace I leave with you; my peace I give you. I do not give to you as the world gives. Do not let your hearts be troubled and do not be afraid" (John 14:27 NIV). If we do not stand firmly rooted in God's peace, then fear, anxiety, worry, and doubt can overwhelm us. Suddenly we're unsure, then we feel like we're standing on shaky ground.

Do not give the enemy a foothold in your life by stripping away your peace. What unsettles you today? What worries run through your mind? Bring each of those cares before God in prayer and ask Him to fill you with His peace.

Prince of Peace, I come before You now with all my worries and all my fears. I trust in Your sovereign control. Fill me with Your peace so I am protected from the evil assaults of worry, doubt, fear, and anxiety.

Day 338

Shield of Faith

At all times carry faith as a shield; for with it you will be able to put out all the burning arrows shot by the Evil One.

Ephesians 6:16 GNT

In this ongoing spiritual battle, we are to "be alert, be on watch! Your enemy, the Devil, roams around like a roaring lion, looking for someone to devour. Be firm in your faith and resist him" (1 Peter 5:8–9 GNT). Carrying a shield of faith—a determined resolve to trust Jesus—helps us stand firm against the devil and resist his schemes. He shoots burning arrows of doubt straight at you—doubts about God's love, goodness, trustworthiness, and faithfulness. He also tries to shoot arrows of shame at you—thoughts that you aren't good enough, worthy enough, faithful enough. Block those arrows with your shield of faith! Stand firm on God's truth—what's true about Him and about who you are in Christ.

What burning arrows are targeting you today? What verses can you memorize and repeat to shield yourself in faith?

Lord, strengthen my faith so I can stand firm and resist the devil. Show me verses I need to memorize to block Satan's arrows.

Day 339

Helmet of Salvation

Accept God's salvation as your helmet.
Ephesians 6:17 NCV

You cannot resist any attacks from the enemy without salvation. As sinners, we are condemned to die physically and spiritually—being forever separated from God (Romans 6:23). The free gift of God is eternal life through Jesus—but we must accept it (Romans 6:23; 5:16–17). Once you have received salvation from God, then confidently secure your helmet.

The enemy will try to condemn you, shame you, and haunt you with your previous sin. You can resist these attacks by sheltering in the safety of your salvation. "Now there is no condemnation for those who belong to Christ Jesus" (Romans 8:1 NLT). God said, "I have swept your sins away like a cloud. Come back to me; I am the one who saves you" (Isaiah 44:22 GNT). Don't let the enemy knock you out with condemnation. Put on your helmet and rest securely in your salvation.

Lord, thank You for dying for me and gifting me with salvation. Help me not to accept feelings of condemnation and unworthiness but to stand firm in the righteousness You give me.

Day 340

Sword of the Spirit

Take the sword of the Spirit, which is the word of God.
Ephesians 6:17 NCV

Every piece of armor Paul listed so far has been defensive—only aimed at protecting the believer. Until now. The final piece of spiritual armor is our one and only offensive weapon—the Word of God. We are not to go charging against Satan. (Paul clearly stated that our goal in this battle is just to stay standing and hold our ground.) But of all the pieces of armor, the sword of the Spirit is how we deal blows to the enemy as we defend our ground. Jesus Himself used God's Word to fend off Satan (Matthew 4:3–11). God's Word is powerful!

How are you feeling tempted or attacked today? What scriptures can you memorize and repeat aloud to help you fight off the enemy? (For help, flip through this devotional and highlight your favorites!)

Holy Father, I praise You for being so strong and mighty. Your Word alone is powerful enough to send the enemy packing. Help me memorize Your Word and use it effectively when Satan attacks me.

Day 341

Choose Real Love and Joy

"I have loved you even as the Father has loved me. Remain in my love. When you obey my commandments, you remain in my love, just as I obey my Father's commandments and remain in his love. I have told you these things so that you will be filled with my joy. Yes, your joy will overflow! This is my commandment: Love each other in the same way I have loved you."

JOHN 15:9–12 NLT

The world around us gives all kinds of bad ideas of what love and joy are. But Jesus tells us in John 15 how to have *real* love and joy. When we obey Jesus the way He obeyed God, we stay close to God. And because God is love (see 1 John 4:8), our whole life is lived in love. When we live in real love, we can't help but be full of real joy because we are living exactly the way God intended when He created us!

Jesus, I want to live in Your real love and be full of the real joy that comes only from choosing You! Amen.

Day 342

Even When at Our Worst

"I tell you, love your enemies. Help and give without expecting a return. You'll never—I promise—regret it. Live out this God-created identity the way our Father lives toward us, generously and graciously, even when we're at our worst. Our Father is kind; you be kind."

Luke 6:35–36 MSG

Scripture tells us that being *at our worst* is no excuse for bad behavior. That means we can't scream at our siblings for hogging the bathroom when we're running late or be rude to a teammate for missing the shot that would've won the game. Waking up cranky doesn't give us a free pass to be dismissive to our parents. And a bad test grade doesn't justify being rude to the teacher.

Instead—no matter how we feel—God wants us to live generously. He wants us to be gracious in our responses. We're to help and give, even to those we're in conflict with. And KINDNESS should be our default button. Yes, friend, the Lord wants us to choose love without fail.

Lord, there is no excuse for treating others badly. Help me always choose love. Amen.

Day 343

East to West

As far as the east is from the west, so far has
He removed our wrongdoings from us.
PSALM 103:12 NASB

If you're traveling west, you can't be going east at the same time. You'll continue moving west until you switch directions. East and west will never touch each other.

If your hope is in Jesus, then God has completely removed your sins and taken them to a place where they can't haunt you with shame, guilt, and regret.

Not only are your sins forgiven and removed from you, but they continue moving away as the Lord leads you westward into His waiting salvation.

Dear God, You've shown me such incredible mercy by taking my sins and removing them completely. Help me move forward and rest in Your forgiveness.

Day 344

Don't Judge

Do not speak against one another, brothers and sisters. The one who speaks against a brother or sister, or judges his brother or sister, speaks against the law and judges the law; but if you judge the law, you are not a doer of the law but a judge of it.

JAMES 4:11 NASB

Let's face it. People are annoying sometimes. They can be selfish, self-centered, and mean. Sometimes they're just plain weird. And before we go any further, let's just admit that if you're reading this, you fall into the *people* category.

Since we all mess up, we really don't have a right to judge each other. We're all on our own journeys with God, and He wants us to love and encourage each other. He doesn't want us to make others feel ashamed or condemned. It's not our job to be the Holy Spirit and convict people's hearts. When someone seems off or they annoy you, remember to show them the same grace God shows you every single day.

Forgive me for judging others, Lord.
Show me how to love them.

Day 345

Posture of Prayer

And pray in the Spirit on all occasions with all kinds of prayers and requests. With this in mind, be alert and always keep on praying for all the Lord's people.
EPHESIANS 6:18 NIV

So we've put on the full armor of God. Next, Paul described the attitude and posture we should continually maintain. We need to be prayerful and alert at all times. Attacks are imminent, from a crafty and cunning enemy. God's power and wisdom are needed as we navigate this ongoing warfare. Paul emphasized this vital need to pray at all times and with persistence and intensity. A nuclear war cannot be won with bows and arrows. Likewise, spiritual battles cannot be won with human effort. Prayer is our access to God's power and also keeps us alert to the spiritual dangers around us.

Regularly examine your armor. Does any piece need attention or repair? As you stand defensively against the enemy, stay alert and in prayer so you can confidently shout, "Not today, Satan!"

Lord, please guide me with Your wisdom, warning me of spiritual dangers. I also pray for. . .

Day 346

Different Gifts from the Same God

There are different kinds of spiritual gifts,
but they all come from the same Spirit. There are
different ways to serve the same Lord, and we can
each do different things. Yet the same God works
in all of us and helps us in everything we do.
1 CORINTHIANS 12:4–6 CEV

Our world would be so dull if everyone had the same personalities, abilities, and talents! The Bible talks about how the Holy Spirit gives different gifts to each of His people, different ways to serve Jesus, different ways to help one another. God has blessed us all with unique talents and individual abilities to do what He asks us to do. It's so important to never compare and expect other Christians to be exactly like us. God purposefully made us different, with tasks designed specifically for us. We can let Him show us what they are and then do them for His glory!

Jesus, thank You for my unique gifts. Help me to know how and when to use them like You want me to. Amen.

Day 347

Being Bold Anyway

"What blessings await you when people hate you and exclude you and mock you and curse you as evil because you follow the Son of Man."
LUKE 6:22 NLT

Don't be shy about your faith. Instead, boldly walk it out without apology. Offer to pray for someone who's hurting. Thank God before you eat your lunch. Be willing to tell your testimony when the opportunity arises. Share powerful scriptures with others. Blare worship music when you feel like it. Choose to love those around you, just as God commands. And if people treat you badly for it, know you are blessed.

There will be times your faith offends people. They won't like what you stand for and may be vocal about it. They may even alienate you, trying to make you feel alone and unloved. Let this only strengthen you through the Lord because you're able to see the bigger picture. The truth is you're fully and completely loved, so let compassion flow out.

Lord, give me the courage I need to shine Your light for others to see, even if they respond in hateful ways. Amen.

Day 348

Imprisoned for the Gospel

Remember the prisoners, as though in prison with them, and those who are badly treated, since you yourselves also are in the body.

HEBREWS 13:3 NASB

Consider the human body for a moment. When one part of your body hurts—even something as small as a stubbed little toe—your whole body is aware of it.

All around the world, members of Christ's body are mistreated or imprisoned for following Him. We're given two powerful weapons to help our persecuted brothers and sisters: prayer and encouragement. We can take hurting believers before God in prayer and ask Him to rescue them. In some cases, we can send letters of encouragement to those imprisoned and remind them that they're loved and not forgotten.

Dear Lord, comfort and help those suffering for Your name, and free those imprisoned because of their belief in You.

Day 349

Who You Are

Let us then approach God's throne of grace with confidence, so that we may receive mercy and find grace to help us in our time of need.

HEBREWS 4:16 NIV

Remember that time you walked in on the king of England without even knocking and he acted so glad to see you? Unless you are a member of his immediate family, you probably *don't* have that memory. Anyone else who barged into the king's presence would be arrested.

But we can approach God's throne anytime we want because—you guessed it!—we're His children. He loves us, and He's always glad to see us. When we need something, He *wants* us to come to Him. He *wants* us to tell Him all about it so He can fix it for us—or at least help us through it.

Next time something is on your mind, remember who you are. Approach your Father with confidence, knowing He loves you beyond measure.

I'm so glad I'm Your child. Thank You for always welcoming me, always listening, and always showing me Your love.

Day 350

See Ya, Satan!

Submit yourselves, then, to God.
Resist the devil, and he will flee from you.
JAMES 4:7 NIV

Satan is your number one enemy in this life. If you're on God's team, then the devil is going to attack you. He wants to steal, kill, and destroy any of God's blessings in your life (John 10:10). Should we be afraid of Satan? No! God has defeated him, and he's not nearly as powerful as Jesus. Should we be aware of Satan and his fighting tactics? Yes. So wear your spiritual armor and take your stand against the enemy's schemes. You can have total confidence that as you wear your armor and submit to God, Satan will run away from you. He's no match for Jesus!

Examine your life. Where is the enemy attempting to steal, kill, and destroy? Is he stealing your joy? Attempting to destroy a relationship through miscommunication and division? Killing your confidence? Submit to God, and make that evil scumbag skedaddle!

> Jesus, I submit myself to You. I choose to be on Your team and let You be the captain. Help me recognize Satan's attacks and resist them.

Day 351

Roots

"But blessed is the one who trusts in the LORD, whose confidence is in him. They will be like a tree planted by the water that sends out its roots by the stream. It does not fear when heat comes; its leaves are always green. It has no worries in a year of drought and never fails to bear fruit."

JEREMIAH 17:7–8 NIV

Have you ever noticed how big the trees grow down by the river? The fresh, flowing water nourishes the roots, causing them to grow strong and tall. What a great comparison for us. When we trust in God, that faith nourishes our roots. That confidence in Him causes us to be strong and stand firm when tough times come.

That tree has plenty of water even in times of drought—after all, the roots run deep in the ground to the water source. We will face drought and difficulties in our lives too. But our roots of faith run deep and connect us to our source of life.

I trust You alone for everything I need, Lord.

Day 352

Watch Out for Those Who Leave Jesus Out

Be careful that no one changes your mind and faith by much learning and big sounding ideas. Those things are what men dream up. They are always trying to make new religions. These leave out Christ. For Christ is not only God-like, He is God in human flesh. When you have Christ, you are complete. He is the head over all leaders and powers. When you became a Christian, you were set free from the sinful things of the world.

COLOSSIANS 2:8–11 NLV

Any teaching of this world about faith that excludes Jesus is false religion, a waste of time. Our faith in Jesus depends on the fact that He alone is the risen Savior who conquered death and paid the price for our sin. First Corinthians 15:17, 19–20 (CEV) says, "Unless Christ was raised to life, your faith is useless, and you are still living in your sins. . . . If our hope in Christ is good only for this life, we are worse off than anyone else. But Christ has been raised to life!"

Jesus, You are alive, and I praise You! You alone are the one true risen Savior; You alone are worthy of faith! Help me watch for and avoid any teaching that leaves You out! Amen.

Day 353

Keep Loving Them

"To you who are willing to listen, I say, love your enemies! Do good to those who hate you. Bless those who curse you. Pray for those who hurt you."
LUKE 6:27–28 NLT

Today's verses are echoing a command that's mentioned several times in the Word. God is clear when He tells us to love our enemies regardless of what they do. If they hate you, love them. If they treat you like dirt, love them. If they turn others against you, love them. If they ruin your reputation or damage your relationships, love them. If their words are full of profanity toward you, love them. Even more, pray for them.

Friend, this is a hard path to walk unless you are clinging to God for strength and might. Only through Him can you find the confidence needed to stand strong no matter what. Cry out to the Lord and watch as He blesses your obedience.

Lord, come close to me and strengthen me to love my enemies no matter what they do. I'm desperate for Your help. Amen.

Day 354

All Things for Good

And we know that for those who love God all things work together for good, for those who are called according to his purpose.

Romans 8:28 ESV

For unbelievers, bad circumstances are simply bad circumstances. When you follow Christ, however, life's difficulties become an opportunity for God to display His power and faithfulness.

What Satan uses to try to destroy your faith, God spins into spiritual gold. He uses hardships to perfect your faith, grow your character, and strengthen your foundation so your hope lies in Him and not in the things of the world.

Dear God, You know that life brings a lot of ups and downs. It's a gift to know that even the bad things are worked for my good. Help me trust You and remember this promise when things get tough.

Day 355

Confidence Killer

Pay careful attention to your own work, for then you will get the satisfaction of a job well done, and you won't need to compare yourself to anyone else. For we are each responsible for our own conduct.

Galatians 6:4–5 NLT

You wanna know the best way to have confidence? Stop comparing yourself to others. There will *always* be someone prettier than you, more fashionable than you, smarter than you, more athletic than you. . .and on and on and on. Stop trying to achieve some impossible standard. Put on blinders and just look at yourself. Are you doing the best *you* can do? Don't sell yourself short. If you know you can try harder, do it. If you can be proud of what you've accomplished because you gave it your absolute best, then that's enough.

Comparison is an automatic confidence killer. So when you're tempted to measure yourself against someone else, chuck that thought and be proud of who God made *you* to be!

Lord, it's so easy to lose my confidence when I'm comparing myself to others. Help me do my best and be satisfied with that.

Day 356

The Source

But remember the L*ORD your God, for it is he who gives you the ability to produce wealth, and so confirms his covenant, which he swore to your ancestors, as it is today.*

DEUTERONOMY 8:18 NIV

In this chapter, Moses warns the Israelites against pride. He reminds them that God hates pride, and He won't bless people who think they can do things without God's help. When we accomplish things, it's easy to get all puffed up and take the credit. But God is the one who gives us our abilities. We may have aced that test, but God gave us a good mind so we could learn. We may have made the varsity team or landed the lead in the school play, but those abilities also come from God.

He wants us to be good stewards of what He's given us. He likes it when we work hard to develop our gifts and talents. But we must never forget the source of every good gift—God.

Thank You for everything You've given me, Father. Help me honor You with all of it.

Day 357

Thirsting for God

As the deer pants for streams of water, so my soul pants for you, my God. My soul thirsts for God, for the living God. When can I go and meet with God?

Psalm 42:1–2 NIV

Have you ever felt yourself thirst for God? Think about how you feel after a long, hot day outside. Do you feel that same parched feeling but know that only God can quench your thirst?

When you spend your time focusing on things of the world, it's easy to feel depleted. Yet God is the one to quench your thirst. He's the one who will refresh you and your thirsty soul.

Instead of looking for ways you can feel temporarily satisfied with temporary, earthly pursuits, seek the Lord. Meet with Him, either with your Bible or prayer or both, and watch the way He refreshes you.

I thirst for You, God. I'm tired of all the quick fixes this world offers, because they're so fleeting. Please satisfy my thirst for You!

Day 358

Open My Eyes

Do good to me, your servant, so I can live, so I can obey your word. Open my eyes to see the miracles in your teachings.

Psalm 119:17–18 NCV

You don't always know what the Lord is doing in your life. In fact, it might take years to figure out the ways He is working. And in some situations, you'll never understand.

When you're feeling particularly puzzled about what's going on, pray that the Lord will open your eyes to see.

It's also essential to ask Him to open your eyes to see the miracles found in His teachings in His Word. Ask Him to do good to you if it means that you will obey His Word. Read His Word so you can understand and obey it, and wait for Him to open your eyes to see the miracles in His teachings.

Father, please open my eyes to see the miracles in Your teachings. Please help me obey Your Word.

Day 359

Nathanael and Jesus

As they approached, Jesus said, "Now here is a genuine son of Israel—a man of complete integrity." "How do you know about me?" Nathanael asked. Jesus replied, "I could see you under the fig tree before Philip found you." Then Nathanael exclaimed, "Rabbi, you are the Son of God—the King of Israel!" Jesus asked him, "Do you believe this just because I told you I had seen you under the fig tree? You will see greater things than this."

John 1:47–50 NLT

Jesus described Nathanael as a man of complete integrity. What a compliment from the only one who knows everything! Still, Nathanael needed to change his life to love and follow Jesus, just like we all do! It's wonderful to be a good and kind person, but even the most moral and nicest people still need to choose Jesus as Savior.

Jesus, help me remind myself and show others that being kind and full of integrity is wonderful, but even the best-behaved people still need to choose You as Savior. Amen.

Day 360

God Promises to Bless Us

The Lord *will grant you abundant prosperity—in the fruit of your womb, the young of your livestock and the crops of your ground—in the land he swore to your ancestors to give you.*

Deuteronomy 28:11 NIV

Here, Moses talks to the Israelites about obedience. He reminds them of the benefits of honoring God and doing what He says. God's promises to the Israelites are the same promises He makes to all His children. We're included!

Some of God's blessings benefit everyone, like rain and air and pretty flowers. But God saves an extra level of blessing for those who honor Him, obey Him, and trust Him. Though we will still have troubles, we'll also experience peace and joy that the rest of the world doesn't understand. He loves to bless His children who love Him.

Father, I want Your blessings. Teach me to be obedient and to honor You with everything in my life.

Day 361

Fear Factor

For God has not given us a spirit of fear and timidity, but of power, love, and self-discipline.
2 Timothy 1:7 NLT

Fear. It's everywhere. Fear of getting sick. Fear of not being accepted. Fear of the future. The enemy uses fear to sideline us. Satan wants to cause such an interruption in our lives that we stop playing the game. Because what does fear do? It paralyzes us. We stop trusting God. We no longer do what God wants us to do because we're so afraid.

But that's not how God wants us to live! When we live in fear, we've taken our eyes off God and focused on the problem. We need to fix our eyes on Jesus and stay confident in who He is and His promises to us. You can walk in confidence, power, and love because you know God is sovereign, He is always with you, He is good and fair, and He loves you. When you are tempted to be afraid, remember: Don't let your fear be bigger than your God!

Almighty Father, You alone are the most powerful in the universe. Forgive me for nurturing fear and not trusting You.

Day 362

When You Feel Like Quitting

Christ gives me the strength to face anything.
PHILIPPIANS 4:13 CEV

Have you ever just wanted to immediately quit something you're involved in? We've all been there. But when we do finish something without quitting in the middle of it, we can usually look back and see how Jesus was giving us just what we needed to take things one day at a time. And hopefully, we can see how He used that time to grow us into better, stronger people because we pushed through with commitment and endurance instead of giving up. In any hard situation, be sure to call on Jesus for help; then, trust in Him and wait on Him. He will either help you walk through it day by day until it's over or help you find a wise way out ASAP.

Jesus, please help me when I want to quit in the middle of hard circumstances. Please give me endurance, strength, courage, and wisdom. And please help me find joy in the midst of the struggle too. Amen.

Day 363

All the Time

A friend loves at all times, and a brother is born for adversity.
PROVERBS 17:17 NASB

Have you heard of a fair-weather friend? That's someone who cares about you when things are good. . .but when things get tough, that person disappears. According to this verse, that person isn't a friend at all.

A friend loves all the time. They celebrate with you in the good times and cry with you in the bad. They stand by you when nobody else does. We expect our family members to stand with us—a brother or sister will help you through difficult times. But a true friend will do that too.

If someone says they're your friend but talks about you behind your back or pretends they don't know you when certain people are around, don't waste your time. Be polite. Be kind. But look for another friend. And always strive to be the kind of steady, consistent friend who loves others in good times and bad.

Bring me true friends, Lord.
And help me be a devoted friend to others.

Day 364

Love and Hate

If someone says, "I love God," and yet he hates his brother or sister, he is a liar; for the one who does not love his brother and sister whom he has seen, cannot love God, whom he has not seen.

1 JOHN 4:20 NASB

Earlier in this chapter, John tells us that God is love. The word *is* is like an equal sign. Think about that. God isn't just *loving*. God = love.

If God lives in our hearts, then His love lives there. Just as light extinguishes darkness, love destroys hate. The two cannot exist together. If we say we love God but hate another person, we're mistaken. Hate cannot live in the same space as God.

If you struggle to love someone, talk to God. Tell Him you're trying and that you need His help. He doesn't expect you to do the hard things on your own. He will heal your heart, help you forgive, and replace hate with love. . .if you let Him.

I don't want to hate anyone, Lord. Replace the hate with Your love.

Day 365

Power Up!

I also pray that you will understand the incredible greatness of God's power for us who believe him. This is the same mighty power that raised Christ from the dead and seated him in the place of honor at God's right hand in the heavenly realms.

Ephesians 1:19–20 NLT

The same power that raised Christ from the dead is in you. Let that sink in. The *same power* that *raised Christ from the dead* is in *YOU*! His power fills us with endurance, patience, and joy (Colossians 1:11). It turns our weakness into strength (2 Corinthians 12:9–10). It gives us boldness to share Jesus with our family members, friends, and strangers (Acts 1:8). His power frees us from sin (Romans 6:6).

How have you been living powerless when you could be powerful? How do you need to tap into God's power? Ask God to help you understand the incredible greatness of His power and how He wants you to live in that power today.

Mighty God, I cannot even begin to grasp the fullness of Your power that lives in me. Help me live in that power for the glory of Your name.

Scripture Index

OLD TESTAMENT

Genesis

1:27 .... Day 232
2:2–3 .... Day 236
3:4–5 .... Day 282
4:26 .... Day 8
15:1–3 .... Day 80
15:6 .... Day 86
15:7–8 .... Day 91
16:13 .... Days 73, 196
17:1–3 .... Day 204
24:12–14 .... Day 314
24:26–27 .... Day 320
40:14 .... Day 24
50:20 .... Day 268

Exodus

3:11 .... Day 87
3:13–14 .... Day 22
5:22–23 .... Day 254
15:26 .... Day 69
20:2 .... Day 83
22:27 .... Day 64
23:22 .... Day 271
33:11–13 .... Day 266
34:6 .... Day 59

Leviticus

19:17 .... Day 92

Deuteronomy

8:18 .... Day 356
28:11 .... Day 360

Joshua

1:9 .... Day 33
10:12–13 .... Day 176

Judges

16:28 .... Day 141
21:25 .... Day 312

Ruth

1:16 .... Day 284

1 Samuel

1:10–11 .... Day 302

2 Samuel

22:1–4 .... Day 173

1 Chronicles

4:10 .... Days 39, 169
16:35–36 .... Day 227
17:19 .... Day 292

Ezra

9:6........................ Day 211

Nehemiah

1:4–5...................... Day 66
9:6........................ Day 50

Psalms

3:1–3...................... Day 247
4:1........................ Day 37
4:8........................ Day 293
5:4–6...................... Day 71
6:1–3...................... Day 216
8:3–4...................... Day 164
9:10....................... Day 197
16:1–2..................... Day 240
18:3....................... Day 161
23......................... Day 102
23:4....................... Day 133
25:8....................... Day 32
25:11...................... Day 74
26:2–3..................... Day 205
28:1–2..................... Day 217
30:5....................... Day 220
32:5....................... Day 260
34:17–18................... Day 120
35:1....................... Day 272
36:5–6..................... Day 283
36:7....................... Day 289
37:4....................... Day 185
37:4–7..................... Day 317
37:23–24................... Day 313
38:9–11.................... Day 308
40:2–3..................... Day 311
40:11 .... Day 61
42:1–2..................... Day 357
42:5....................... Day 231
43:3....................... Day 181
46:1–3..................... Day 78
50:15...................... Day 23
55:22...................... Day 106
56:3....................... Day 40
56:8....................... Day 199
63:1–4..................... Day 115
66:17–19................... Day 54
71:5....................... Day 17
73:25–26................... Day 11
100........................ Day 124
101:3–4.................... Day 112
103:12......... Days 203, 343
109:26..................... Day 42
115:1...................... Day 127
118:5–7.................... Day 166
119:17–18.................. Day 358
119:50..................... Day 208

119:73 .... Day 152
139:1–4 .... Day 99
139:7–8, 11–12 .... Day 221
139:13–16 .... Day 239
143:7–8 .... Day 126
143:8 .... Day 18

Proverbs

1:8 .... Day 328
3:5, 7 .... Day 296
10:12 .... Day 116
13:20 .... Day 251
15:1 .... Day 183
16:9 .... Day 263
17:17 .... Days 182, 363
24:16 .... Day 300
24:17 .... Day 281
25:21–22 .... Day 195
27:6 .... Day 79
31:26 .... Day 6

Ecclesiastes

7:9 .... Day 187

Isaiah

9:6–7 .... Day 97
26:3 .... Days 137, 225
30:15 .... Day 4
41:10 .... Day 27
43:1 .... Day 193
43:13 .... Day 226
44:22 .... Day 209
53:4–5 .... Day 49
54:17 .... Day 89

Jeremiah

1:4–8 .... Day 36
8:4 .... Day 295
17:7–8 .... Intro, 351
29:11 .... Day 144
32:16–17 .... Day 255

Lamentations

3:22–23 .... Day 331

Jonah

2:1–3 .... Day 121
4:6 .... Day 163

Micah

6:8 .... Day 76

Habakkuk

1:2 .... Day 325

Malachi

3:6 .... Day 26

NEW TESTAMENT

Matthew

1:18–21, 24 .... Day 95
1:23.............. Days 93, 103
3:1–3.................... Day 130
4:4........................ Day 329
4:18–22................ Day 136
5:3–12.................. Day 118
5:11........................ Day 84
5:14–16......... Days 77, 301
5:43–44................ Day 142
5:45...................... Day 147
6:8........................ Day 250
6:25–27................ Day 286
6:27–30................ Day 291
6:33...................... Day 180
7:2.......................... Day 90
7:15–16, 20 .... Day 299
10:26, 28 .... Day 280
10:29–31............. Day 269
11:28.................... Day 249
13:10...................... Day 82
13:44.................... Day 167
16:13–16............. Day 172
17:5...................... Day 324
18:6...................... Day 319
18:21–22............. Day 237
20:28.................... Day 191
21:21.................... Day 238
22:36–38............. Day 158
22:36–39................ Day 44
22:39.................... Day 159
26:41.................... Day 327
26:42.................... Day 210
28:20...................... Day 45

Mark

1:35–37................ Day 322
2:9–12.................. Day 207
6:55–56................ Day 155
9:24...................... Day 194
10:14–15............. Day 257
10:17, 20–23 .... Day 275
11:23.................... Day 246
12:29–30............. Day 122
12:31.................... Day 128
12:42.................... Day 184
12:42–44............. Day 326
16:15.................... Day 229

Luke

1:30–31 .... Day 94
5:5–7.................... Day 287

5:27–28................ Day 277
5:27–32................ Day 160
6:22...................... Day 347
6:27–28....... Days 276, 353
6:35–36................ Day 342
9:23........................ Day 16
10:36–37.............. Day 298
10:38–39.............. Day 151
11:2–4........... Days 28, 188
11:5–9.................... Day 29
11:11–13................ Day 30
15:13.................... Day 201
19:3...................... Day 332
23:42–43.............. Day 316

John

1:1, 14.................. Day 107
1:1–3, 14................ Day 72
1:12...................... Day 186
1:47–50................ Day 359
2:24...................... Day 202
3:16................ Days 7, 309
4:50........................ Day 57
6:32–35................ Day 148
6:35...................... Day 113
8:12...................... Day 119
9:1–7.................... Day 170
10:7, 9–10............ Day 125
10:10.................... Day 132
10:11.................... Day 131
11:25.................... Day 138
11:41–44.............. Day 243
13:12–17.............. Day 224
13:34...................... Day 75
13:35............ Days 81, 242
14:1–4.................. Day 230
14:6...................... Day 145
14:15.................... Day 174
14:26...................... Day 21
14:27.................... Day 149
15:1, 5.................. Day 150
15:9–12................ Day 341
15:12–13................ Day 52
15:13...................... Day 53
15:15–16.............. Day 215
16:33.................... Day 139
17:11........................ Day 9

Acts

4:29–30.................. Day 58
9:1, 3–4................ Day 305

Romans

1:5–6.................... Day 245
1:20........................ Day 55
3:22–25.................. Day 10

3:23.......................... Day 3
5:8......................... Day 154
5:17........................ Day 15
8:18...................... Day 333
8:28............ Days 192, 354
8:37...................... Day 264
8:38–39................ Day 198
12:2...................... Day 256
12:4–5.................. Day 261
12:9............ Days 123, 248
12:10.................... Day 267
12:11.................... Day 177
12:14.................... Day 273
12:15............ Days 13, 278
12:16............ Days 47, 288
12:17.......... Days 265, 297
12:18.................... Day 303
12:19.................... Day 315
12:19–20.............. Day 285
12:20.................... Day 321
12:21.......... Days 274, 330
13:8...................... Day 228
13:10.................... Day 235
15:33.................... Day 109

1 Corinthians

12:4–6.................. Day 346
13:5...................... Day 307
13:8.......................... Day 1
13:13...................... Day 70
15:33.................... Day 259

2 Corinthians

4:8–9.......... Days 108, 306
4:17–18................ Day 290
5:17............ Days 143, 179

Galatians

5:22–23.................. Day 25
6:2.......................... Day 41
6:4–5.................... Day 355

Ephesians

1:4........................ Day 258
1:19–20................ Day 365
2:10...................... Day 252
3:17–19................ Day 111
3:19–21................ Day 310
4:2–3.................... Day 168
4:22–24................ Day 270
4:26–27................ Day 279
4:31–32................ Day 175
5:16...................... Day 262
6:1–3.................... Day 323
6:10–13................ Day 334
6:14............ Days 335, 336
6:15...................... Day 337

6:16 .... Day 338
6:17 .... Days 339, 340
6:18 .... Day 345

Philippians

1:6 .... Day 156
2:3 .... Day 129
2:14 .... Days 56, 135
4:6–7 .... Day 46
4:13 .... Days 105, 362
4:19 .... Day 214

Colossians

2:8–11 .... Day 352
3:12 .... Days 20, 35
3:12–13 .... Day 318
3:13 .... Days 34, 43
3:14 .... Day 48

1 Thessalonians

4:11 .... Day 62
5:18 .... Day 178

2 Timothy

1:7 .... Days 51, 361
2:23–24 .... Day 60
3:15–17 .... Day 38

Titus

3:1–2 .... Day 65

Hebrews

4:16 .... Day 349
7:26–27 .... Day 63
10:19–22 .... Day 162
10:23–25 .... Day 68
10:24 .... Day 67
12:6 .... Day 304
13:2 .... Day 222
13:3 .... Day 348
13:5 .... Days 171, 190

James

1:6 .... Day 233
1:12 .... Day 114
1:26 .... Day 12
2:2–4 .... Day 101
2:13 .... Day 117
2:23 .... Day 5
3:16 .... Day 253
4:7 .... Day 350
4:11 .... Day 344
5:16 .... Day 31

1 Peter

1:6–7 .... Day 104
4:8 .... Day 19
4:10 .... Day 85
4:12–13 .... Day 98

4:14...................... Day 213

1 John

2:3–6..................... Day 165
3:1................. Days 88, 189
3:6........................ Day 200
3:10–11................ Day 206
3:16...................... Day 212
3:18............ Days 218, 294
3:22...................... Day 244
3:23...................... Day 223
4:4........................ Day 219
4:7........................ Day 146
4:7–8........................ Day 2
4:8.......................... Day 14
4:16...................... Day 241
4:18...................... Day 134
4:19........................ Day 96
4:20............ Days 100, 364
4:21...................... Day 110

Jude

24–25................... Day 140

Revelation

1:4–5.................... Day 157
4:8........................ Day 234
4:11...................... Day 153